A Screenwriter's Book Written for Real Writers

Stephen Geller recognizes that the toughest part of writing a screenplay is the writing itself. You can learn the camera angles, the language, and format of a film script, but without playable dialogue, fully developed characters, and a compelling story, you won't get very far.

In *Screenwriting*, Geller addresses the problems that you as a dramatic writer face: How to motivate yourself to work... How to visualize your ideas and put them into words... How to give your characters a chance to develop and your story a chance to come alive... How, in short, to get your idea out of your head and into the movie theatre.

Geller says:

"Writing is not a secure profession. (I laugh as I write this line.) Screenwriting even less. But if you are mad enough to inflict your dreams upon the unsuspecting public, then learn to inflict them well, and control the direction of the infliction."

Bantam Books of Related Interest
Ask your bookseller for the books you have missed

HOW TO BE A FREELANCE WRITER
    by David Martindale
THE WRITER'S SURVIVAL MANUAL by Carol Meyer
WRITING IN GENERAL AND THE SHORT STORY IN
    PARTICULAR by Rust Hills
WRITING AND RESEARCHING TERM PAPERS AND
    REPORTS by Eugene Ehrlich and Daniel Murphy
THE BUSINESS WRITING HANDBOOK
    by William C. Paxson
30 WAYS TO HELP YOU WRITE by Fran Weber Shaw
HOW TO ACHIEVE COMPETENCE IN ENGLISH
    by Eric W. Johnson
THE BANTAM BOOK OF CORRECT LETTER WRITING
THE SCRIBNER-BANTAM ENGLISH DICTIONARY

QUANTITY PURCHASES

Companies, professional groups, churches, clubs
and other organizations may qualify for special
terms when ordering 24 or more copies of this
title. For information, contact the Direct Response
Department, Bantam Books, 666 Fifth Avenue,
New York, N.Y. 10103. Phone (212) 765-6500.

Screenwriting:
A Method

Stephen Geller

BANTAM BOOKS
TORONTO • NEW YORK • LONDON • SYDNEY • AUCKLAND

SCREENWRITING: A METHOD
A Bantam Book / April 1985

All rights reserved.
Copyright © 1984 by Stephen Geller.
Cover artwork copyright © 1985 by Bantam Books, Inc.
This book may not be reproduced in whole or in part, by
mimeograph or any other means, without permission.
For information address: Bantam Books, Inc.

ISBN 0-553-24110-9

Published simultaneously in the United States and Canada

Bantam Books are published by Bantam Books, Inc. Its trademark, consisting of the words "Bantam Books" and the por-
trayal of a rooster, is Registered in U.S. Patent and Trademark
Office and in other countries. Marca Registrada. Bantam
Books, Inc., 666 Fifth Avenue, New York, New York 10103.

PRINTED IN THE UNITED STATES OF AMERICA

O   0 9 8 7 6 5 4 3 2 1

To Charlie Chaplin, Walt Disney,
Buster Keaton, W.C. Fields—giants of
the past,
to Federico Fellini, Ingmar Bergman,
Woody Allen—giants of the present,
and to all baby writer-director giants,
growing into the future,
this book is dedicated.

I wish to thank Maurice Rapf of the Film Studies Program at Dartmouth College for allowing me to make sense of my own film experience before many patient and unsuspecting students of Drama 58; my literary agent, Michael Carlisle, for realizing that many of the ideas might make sense to others; my editor, LuAnn Walther, who helped shape the ungainly into the presentable; Janice Kyd, who never complained about retyping Shakespeare; and my immediate family, as well as my extended family at Bar Cola di Rienzo in Rome, where the book finally was written.

Part One:
Idea + Force + Form

By Way of Introduction...

In the past decade dozens of books about screenwriting have been published. From highly abstract and theoretical texts to the most complex nuts-and-bolts blueprints, the film student, beginning screenwriter or, simply, the interested reader has been barraged by this volley of well-intended advice.

Yet nearly all the texts have committed one basic error:

They have assumed that a screenwriter is a special breed, a combination scribe-Slavic art theoretician-geometry whiz and, of course, an expert in French film criticism. If one had to define screenwriters by the works written for their professional aid and comfort, one would have a curious time coming to any meaningful conclusion.

For few texts assume that the screenwriter is, above everything else, a writer.

And fewer texts assume that the screenwriter also can write novels and poetry and plays and—surprise!—criticism. Sadly, many screenwriters have begun to believe this illogical assumption, thereby cutting themselves off from their own legitimate roots: dramatic literature.

Screenwriting: A Method is a not-so-very-humble attempt to recast and rebalance the screenwriter's art; to demonstrate that the screenplay is a cousin to theater, and a little brother to the novel; that the screenplay *is* an art

• 3

form, indeed, and without which cinema screens would be whiter-than-white.

For the past sixteen years I have earned my living as a screenwriter.

In many respects, I feel fortunate: first, I would rather be writing than doing most anything else. Second, much of that "anything else" is traveling, and meeting people in professions other than the film business. Screenwriting has allowed me to travel and, in the course of research, to meet precisely those people who would interest me—even if I hadn't been hired to write about them.

I also write novels.

Screenwriting affords me the money to buy the time to write those novels.

Implied here, of course, is the idea that I would prefer to write novels than screenplays. That is both true and untrue. If I've an idea whose rhythm demands a novelistic approach, then a novel it becomes. If, on the other hand, I've an idea whose rhythm depends upon a succession of sensual images, then a film it becomes.

I can think of dozens of others who are no different from me: novelists, playwrights, and poets who also write screenplays.

Simply, a writer writes.

With the force and the form best suited to the idea.

This book, therefore, will make no attempt to separate the screenplay from its literary and dramatic roots. The desire to capture the appropriate image defining character, emotional state or place is the province of every writer.

Only the form differs.

And form is the least of the writer's problems.

Form can be taught.

Give me fifteen minutes of your reading time, and I will teach you all you need to know about the form of the screenplay.

Why?

Because it's simple.

Admittedly, most film students or writers who attempt screenplays are overwhelmed by "film vocabulary." It has become a burgeoning side-industry, keeping film critics and writers of how-to books alive and well.

I am for everybody being alive and well. But I also believe in an honest day's work.

My concern in this process of screenwriting, therefore, has less to do with form than it has to do with saving what has become one of the most neglected aspects of the screenplay, and certainly the most endangered species in cinema:

Character

During the last decade, American film-making has grown as technically dazzling as it has withered in memorable characters and content. Ingenious special effects, wondrous camera angles, decor, and atmosphere seem to have comprised the vast part of our entertainment. Film perhaps to have become a tale told by an idiot, full of Dolby sound and furious special effects, and signifying nothing.

Strangely enough, much of this arises from those very places where one would assume character and theme to be all-important: the university and, within it, the film school. Ironically, the emphasis there has been on film technique. In no way am I denigrating an understanding of these techniques. I am attempting, however, to put them in their appropriate place.

No camera angle, subjective use of sound or special

effects will tell a full tale or reveal character. If you do not know who your characters are, no magnificent shot or effect will define them for you.

This book will teach you form, yes.

But, more important, it will start you thinking about character, and make you realize that you are part of a tradition which began long before D. W. Griffith conceived of *Birth of a Nation*.

My experience teaching screenwriting at Dartmouth College has shown me that most students are perfectly capable of absorbing form in a few sessions, but must spend a far greater time asking themselves:

1. Who are the characters in my work?
2. What do they feel and desire? What are their goals? How do they speak?
3. How can I best convey these characters, with all their feelings and desires, to an audience?

From these questions springs the universe of film, novel, play and, sometimes, poem.

What do I mean by character?
People.
Lives.
And learning about other lives through your own ideas of feeling, and your own feeling about ideas.
And where do ideas and feeling lie in uneasy balance, but in people?
Character.

I understand the tragicomic *angst* of an artist through the character of Guido in *8½*. I live the drama of a 19th-century bourgeois family in *Cries and Whispers*. I even know how a flying elephant feels when he is mocked by crows in *Dumbo*.

Fellini, Disney, and Bergman enrich my life by allowing

me to take part in other lives, other universes, and to empathize with those lives.

This book is written with the hope that you will help to save film's most endearing species: character.

For the past sixteen years I have examined every assignment I've accepted as if it were a separate universe, with its own physical laws. The laws, of course, spring from character. My job as screenwriter is to discover those laws, then to make them function well.

To assume that each universe is a genre, and has the same laws as the last galaxy explored is to be both lazy, unadventurous, and unprofessional. The battle will have been lost before it even has had a chance to begin.

Worst of all, it will have made me think of character in cliché terms. Certainly I will not have allowed the new characters (new universe) to come alive and, through their actions, to teach me about themselves. I will not have conveyed fully to you, reader or audience, what they might have conveyed to me, because I was not allowing them to live fully. And our contract, yours and mine, (which is the film ticket, or the price of the novel) will have become a one-sided affair.

People are surprising.

Compulsive. Obsessive.

Comic and grim.

Wondrous, above all.

Here are a few examples of character in action, character which receives our full attention. I will deliberately withhold the names.

See if you can guess the films:

A: I want you to go back and carry on the good work.

L: No thank you, sir.

A: Why not?

L: Well I . . . erm . . . It—erm . . . Let's see now . . . I—killed—two people . . . I mean two Arabs. One was a boy—this was yesterday . . . I led him into a quicksand . . . the other was a man—that was, oh let me see—before Akaba anyway—I had to execute him with my pistol. . . . There was something about it I didn't like.

A: Well naturally.

L: (*Staring into A's face*) No. Something else.

A: I see. (*He looks away—he is uncomfortable*.) Well that's all right; let it be a warning.

L: No. Something else.

A: What then?

L: (*After a pause*) I enjoyed it.

After this brief, ten-line exchange, do you have an idea who "L" is?

Robert Bolt's characterization of T. E. Lawrence, from *Lawrence of Arabia*.

(How many of you remember Robert Bolt? Or did you think of Peter O'Toole and David Lean first?)

The scene is memorable because the *characterization* of Lawrence is memorable.

Guess *this* exchange:

G: I had some trouble with my car. Flat tire. I pulled into your garage till I could get a spare. I thought this was an empty house.

N: It is not. Get out.

G: Wait a minute—haven't I seen you?

N: Or should I call my servant.

G: I know your face. You're N. D. You used to be in pictures. You used to be big.

N: I *am* big. It's the pictures that got small.

Sunset Boulevard, obviously.

Gloria Swanson, certainly.

And each time I have shown that film in class, Norma's line "It's the pictures that got small" gets whoops and applause. Thirty-five years after it was written.

Kudos, as they say in the trades, to Billy Wilder and Charles Brackett—not only for writing nasty-sprightly dialogue, *but for creating a larger-than-life character which Swanson immortalized*.

Let's have another quiz:

J: What's the matter with you, anyway?
S: I'm not very bright, I guess.
J: I wouldn't say that. Careless, maybe.
S: No—just dumb. If I had any brains, I wouldn't be on this crummy train with this crummy girls' band.
J: Then why did you take this job?
S: I used to sing with male bands. But I can't afford it any more.
J: Afford it?
S: Have you ever been with a male band?
J: Me?
S: That's what I'm running away from. I worked with six different ones in the last two years. Oh, brother!
J: Rough?
S: I'll say.
J: You can't trust those guys.
S: I can't trust myself. The moment I'd start with a new band—bingo!

A rap on the knuckles for those of you who didn't guess this scene.

Joe and Sugar, from *Some Like It Hot*.

And, although the emphasis is on Sugar's responses, remember that Joe, escaping from the mob, is asking questions in drag, and all the while Sugar assumes he is female.

Character.

Name one dozen characters who are memorable to you from films of the past decade.

Interestingly, it is not so difficult with films written in the late thirties through the early sixties. Most of the writers in the Industry of those times also worked in different media: Ben Hecht was both a novelist, journalist, and playwright; Nathanael West, Faulkner, and Dorothy Parker were novelists; Garson Kanin a playwright; Budd Schulberg a novelist and essayist; Gore Vidal a playwright, novelist, essayist; Ernest Lehman a short-story writer and publicist.

Each writer brought with him or her the richness of his different worlds and experiences, and a knowledge of theater and of literature.

Directors, during those two decades, were no different: their laboratories were not the film schools but the stage, where the *gradual revelation of character was the core of the dramatic event*.

Elia Kazan, George Roy Hill, Sidney Lumet followed text.

Text rarely followed them.

When their work was most inspired, the text provided the very inspiration.

Working in the theater necessitated coming to terms with the universe of character, conveying its reality to an audience.

Working in film should be no different.

But it is.

The physical tools which should be utilized to help define the universe have become universes unto themselves.

Bad for us.

Help, however, is *not* on its way.

Paradoxically, Help *never left*.

As long as writers are interested in people, and are not browbeaten into assuming that a knowledge of screenplay form and camera angles and special effects is the *sine qua non* of writing; as long as CHARACTER IS ALL, there is yet a chance of exciting the viewer, moving an audience, changing the way others have seen the world.

Wear this trinity upon your sleeve, this magical seal, and you will find the act of writing as pleasurable as it is exciting:

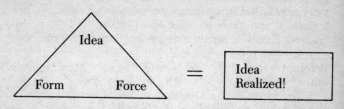

Idea + Force + Form = Idea Realized.

Form

There is nothing occult about the form of a screenplay.
It does not demand a working knowledge of quantum
mechanics or projective geometry.
It is simple.
Breathe easily.
The screenplay form merely requires four elements:

1. Setting description and time of day in which
   the scene is played.
2. Narrative and/or character description.
3. Dialogue.
4. Camera angles *necessary* for the telling of the
   story.

Here is an example of the four elements, unified into
the screenplay form:

1—INTERIOR JET COCKPIT—DAY   1
  CAPTAIN RALPH GIBBS, a sturdy humorless
pilot in his mid-forties, gazes fitfully about the

controls. Frightened, he turns to COPILOT WARREN, a handsome, shiny-eyed dwarf.

> GIBBS
>
> Am I crazy, or are we five hundred feet above Detroit?
>
> WARREN (*Uneasily*)
>
> Do I have to answer *both* questions?

2—EXT. ANDERSON BACKYARD—DAY   2
THE ANDERSON FAMILY—FATHER WILL, MOTHER SYL, DAUGHTER JILL and SON GIL—are seated in a large, wooden swimming pool, happily splashing each other and eating hot dogs. Suddenly their joyous cries are drowned out by the keening of a jet fast approaching them.

> JILL
>
> Duck!
>
> GIL
>
> *Duck* nothing—*plane*!

As the jet screams above the surface of the pool, the FAMILY dives into the water.
UNDERWATER SHOT of the ANDERSON FAMILY, heading for the plug. FATHER WILL struggles with it, surrounded by his anxious brood. He gives the plug a hefty yank. Gesturing for the others to follow, he shimmies into the drain.

3—EXTERIOR PEKING MAIN STREET—LATE AFTERNOON   3
ESTABLISHING SHOT of TWO MILLION BICYCLISTS moving along the splendid avenue. CAMERA TRAVELS THROUGH THE CROWD to an intersection, AND DISCOVERS the ANDERSON FAMILY waiting for the light to change. They still wear their bathing suits, and are dripping wet.

> SYL
>
> Well, here we are in Peking—
>
> FATHER
>
> Looks pretty plane.
>
> GIL

Plane to *you*, *street* to me!

And *that* is the form of the screenplay.
Nothing more.
(Anything less, and you will be left with a blank page.)
Let us examine each of the four basic elements of the screenplay form:

1. Setting Description and Time of Day

These are numbered scenes in capital letters, with the numbers themselves placed on the left- and right-hand margins of the page. In the above examples, there are three Setting/Time of Day Descriptions:

1—INTERIOR JET COCKPIT—DAY	1
2—EXTERIOR ANDERSON BACKYARD—DAY	2
3—EXTERIOR PEKING MAIN STREET—LATE AFTERNOON	3

Although INTERIOR and EXTERIOR often seem redundant (INT. PEKING MAIN STREET would pose some interesting camera and set design problems), they are necessary not only for the budgeting schedule of the film, but also for the clarification of what could be an ambiguous description. Writing 1 (JET COCKPIT—DAY), for example, would *not* tell us whether an internal or external shot was required. Both shots are possible.

TIME OF DAY needs small explanation. If the Andersons are eating hot dogs in their wooden pool at midnight, this would be written:

2—EXTERIOR ANDERSON BACKYARD—MID-NIGHT

The use of the phrase CUT TO between scenes has been deleted from most scripts because the cut is *automatically* implied in a straightforward, chronological narrative. (When, however, simultaneous action in two or three different settings is required, then CROSSCUT TO *occasionally* is used. However, even this phrase is being deleted, for it is becoming apparent to the meanest churl that Scene 2 in fact follows Scene 1, Scene 3 follows Scene 2, etc.) Generaly a writer uses the phrase CROSSCUT TO to ensure that the reader understands that *the event of* Scene 1 (INT. PITTSBURGH TV STATION) is not to be confused with *the event of* Scene 2 (EXT. LATVIAN MOON BASE).

2. Narrative and/or Character Description

John Steinbeck wrote that the hardest chore for him was to write a simple declarative sentence.

If so, then the screenplay is a great test for a writer.

The narrative description of a screenplay consists of a series of simple declarative sentences which the reader easily can follow. The action and description is reduced to absolutely functional prose. Brevity is essential. Two hours of film is an extremely short time. As you will discover, most filmscripts vary in length from 100 to 120 pages. The rule of thumb generally has been:

1 page of script = 1 minute of playing time.

Normally, a half-page of strong physical action will play for longer than thirty seconds, but since all film is *not* strong physical action, the equation, general as it is, functions well.

Keep all descriptions of character and of action simple.

You will need as much space as possible to tell your story.

When your rough draft is 250 pages of brilliant prose, it is not a nice feeling to know that half of it must be consigned to the garbage.

Note the brevity of the descriptions from the example quoted above:

Character Description:
"A sturdy, humorless pilot in his mid-forties";
"A handsome, shiny-eyed dwarf."
Narrative Description:

"He gazes fitfully about the controls. Frightened, he turns to Copilot Warren":
"They are seated in a wooden pool, happily splashing each other and eating hot dogs";
"They are waiting for the light to change."

The descriptions of character and of action are sketched. One paragraph of physical description—*unless the entire film depends upon it*—is a waste of space.

To make the descriptions even more apparent, all NAMES OF CHARACTERS are capitalized. When a production sheet is made, and a budget pulled from the screenplay, then the studio may write:

```
1—INT. JET COCKPIT—DAY—1
   PILOT
   COPILOT  (2)
2—EXT. ANDERSON BACKYARD—DAY—2
   FATHER WILL
   MOTHER SYL  (4)
   SON GIL
   DAUGHTER JILL
3—EXT. PEKING MAIN STREET—DAY—3
   TWO MILLION BICYCLISTS
   ANDERSON FAMILY  (Two Million + 4)
```

By now it should be apparent that the physical form of the screenplay is an extremely refined blueprint, written in simple, clear sentences.

Penance for a steady diet of such writing demands that your Sundays be spent reading Henry James aloud to loved ones.

3. Dialogue

Let us assume that in the past two minutes you have mastered the form of scene, character, and narrative description.

Now the fun may begin.

Dialogue is the gateway to the soul, intellect, and

heart of our structure. Not only does it define our characters and move the events forward, but also it subtly
creates the rhythm of the scenes themselves—*every bit as
much as the images*.

Dialogue is the very texture of character.

(This will be discussed later, and at greater length.)

Since, for the moment, we are concerned solely with
the physical form of the screenplay, let us note that the
physical shape of dialogue within a scene is written as
follows:

1—PHYSICAL SETTING—TIME OF DAY
   Description of CHARACTER or of narrative.

      CHARACTER'S NAME (*Line reading*)
   What the character delights in saying.

        SECOND CHARACTER
  What the second character delights in replying.

Further narrative description, perhaps, or entrance of
ANOTHER CHARACTER, or NEW SCENE.
        And so forth.

Examine the form of the screenplay quoted as you read
this recapitulation:

1. The SETTING/TIME OF DAY are numbered and
   in CAPITAL LETTERS.
2. TWO SPACES between SETTING HEADING and
   Description of Character and Narrative.
3. Description beginning in the margin beneath the
   SETTING.
4. TWO SPACES between the Description and the
   CHARACTER's name.
5. ONE SPACE between the CHARACTER's NAME
   and the dialogue itself.
6. Dialogue compressed in margins smaller than the
   length of the Description line.
7. TWO SPACES after the last line of dialogue, where

either more description occurs, or a NEW SET-
TING begins.

You may have noted the phrase "line reading" after
CHARACTER's NAME. A line reading is a direction for
the performer, telling him how you would wish that particular piece of dialogue to be read. Most performers do not
care to be told by the author how the line is to be read.
Most performers ignore the line reading.

It follows that an angry line is angry, and therefore
needs no line description at all. For example, it is redundant to write:

MR. BOVARY (*Hotly*)
But, Emma, how *could* you?

I admit to using line readings because partly I am a
frustrated director who does not trust directors, and partly
to ensure that some readers *understand* the rhythm and
intention of the scene.

In spite of my optimism, if not self-flattery, however,
most actors still choose to ignore the line readings. Therefore, it is best to make sure that your dialogue is exact and
contains within it the very intention and rhythm you
require. In this fashion the director and performers well
might cater to your rich sensibility.

The least they can do is to veer slightly from your
intention.

The most is to cause permanent mayhem.

(The latter is a particularly nightmarish experience. I
recall several situations where I was particularly indignant
about an actor's delivery of the dialogue and, therefore,
his point-of-view towards the character. "But that's exactly
what you wrote," one director, momentarily confused. "It
may have been what I wrote on the surface, but the *intention*
beneath it was quite different. Don't you ever read the line
directions?" "Oh dear," said the director. "*Those* . . .").

The best rule, therefore, is to define your character
with such precision that anything emerging from his heart
and mind shines with clarity in the dialogue.

Even if your character is behaving ambiguously, let his ambiguity be clear. Let his intention be known.

Intention is simple to define: it is the aim or desire of the character in a scene.

Here is an example of well-defined intention (from *The Graduate*):

MRS. ROBINSON:	Benjamin?
BEN:	Yes?
MRS. ROBINSON:	Will you come over here a minute?
BEN:	Over there?
MRS. ROBINSON:	Yes.
BEN:	Sure.
MRS. ROBINSON:	Will you unzip my dress?

And an example of ill-defined intention (from *The Drop-outs*):

MRS. SMITH:	William?
WILLIAM:	Yes?
MRS. SMITH:	Who played end for the Dallas Cowboys?

4. Camera Directions

In my example of the screenplay form, I have used only two CAMERA DIRECTIONS: an UNDERWATER SHOT, and an ESTABLISHING SHOT which MOVES THROUGH THE CROWD and DISCOVERS the ANDERSONS.

Those particular shots exist because they are essential to the telling of the story.

Without the UNDERWATER SHOT we would not know what happened to the ANDERSONS. Without the ESTABLISHING SHOT we would not know we were in Peking. Without the CAMERA MOVEMENT we would not have linked that shot to the ANDERSON FAMILY (and implying that their drain led right to Peking).

The scene could have been written with a dozen other shots.

And all of them would no doubt have been excised by the director.

The point is very simple:

Write only those shots that are 100% essential to the scene.

When a director reads a script, his principal concern is the story. He doesn't care if you can move a CAMERA through the universe or through your nostrils and into your brain-pan. He wants to know who the characters are, and what happens to them. For example, he himself will decide if the scene in the jet cockpit begins with a TIGHT SHOT of the instrument panel, or a MEDIUM SHOT OF THE PILOT and COPILOT.

And unless those two shots are essential for the storytelling, they have no business wasting what is, for you, page space or story time, precious time indeed.

A device which will capture the attention of those-who-make-things-happen is as follows:

Write your setting. Describe what happens within that setting.

Rush out of that setting, and into the next. If a particular CAMERA SHOT or ANGLE emphasizes *exactly what you want to say*, and even defines it better than words, include it. Otherwise, forget it.

Note also that CAMERA ANGLES, like CHARACTERS' NAMES, are always capitalized. This emphasizes to the reader that you insist the shot is necessary. Bear in mind, however, that if you blithely throw CAMERA ANGLES about the script, ANGLES which have little to do with character revelation or narrative advancement, you will appear both sloppy and amateurish, and ALL IN CAPITAL LETTERS.

(Shortly, I will describe the various types of CAMERA ANGLES and EFFECTS, the grammar of film.)

We are a small fraternity, limited both in time and in talent.

Let us therefore utilize form with the precision of a laser.

Our magical operation also requires two other elements in the process of creation: FORCE and IDEA.

I had stated that FORM is the easiest aspect of our magical seal:

Compared to FORCE and IDEA, you will see why.

Force

How is it possible to address the blank page without fear and loathing and sickness unto death? Certainly many writers publicly have lamented the loneliness of the craft, the Sisyphean labor of filling the page with words both entertaining and profound. Implied in their groans is the desire for approval, from public and/or self. The desire is understandable. Writing is a solitary task indeed. But the groaning is a waste of time.

For example, as of the publication of this text, I have written sixteen screenplays, of which four have been filmed, and thirteen novels, of which four have been published.

Certainly I would prefer all the novels to have been published, and all the screenplays filmed. My consolation, with or without filming and publication, rests in the fact that, in spite of the realities of the marketplace, *I exist as a writer, and enjoy practicing my craft*. Brilliant or boring, mediocre or outrageous as the outcome may be, the act of conceiving a series of characters and living with them as they live, and placing their fluid experiences onto a page is not only exciting, but also harmonious and satisfying. What I have learned is a very simple truth:

Sooner or later the act of writing becomes its own reward.

A blank piece of paper is not the enemy.

It is a mirror of your imagination.

After a time, in that mirror, the shape of character and event comes into focus. Your own curiosity, overwhelmed by enthusiasm, adds force to the shape; enthusiasm swells to delight. The force of witnessed events becomes greater than the force of your will. The characters take over. The force of your work spills into your characters, making *them* become forceful. Energetic. And the force of the characters spills onto the audience—or reader.

How can you *not* write? If someone were to cut off your arms, you would continue with your toes.

How to sustain your initial excitement for your characters?

One: write only about those people and events which interest you.

Since you must live with them for the duration of the writing, you had better enjoy their company. Even if some of them would not make suitable baby sitters for your children, time spent with them might prove illuminating. Interest in your characters gives you the initial force to pursue them as they discover an aspect of their lives. Once alive, the characters themselves will supply the remaining energy.

Professionally I have *never* taken a film assignment I've disliked—even if my financial needs were screaming "Take! Take!" This is not because I am ferociously idealistic; rather, it is because I do not enjoy living with people I dislike. If the idea, book, or project does not stimulate me, does not give me dreams, I would be cheating myself (and the producer, and the publisher) if I pursued the work. Then I would address the blank page with fear and loathing and sickness unto death.

To achieve initial force, therefore, accept only those assignments and/or *write only about those people or events that shake you to your soul*.

Two: how to sustain your initial enthusiasm and force during the long periods of writing?

Here's a painful but pleasurable trick. And it *works*.

In the dramatic narrative, there are innumerable crises, large and small, the "peaks and valleys" of prose.

On Monday, take your characters up to the first peak, the first crisis, *then stop*.

You will, of course, not *wish* to stop. You will wish to see what happens, how the scene resolves.

Instead, listen to music. Take a walk. Cook an interesting pasta. See a film. Forget that your characters are poised on the mountain's edge.

On Tuesday, you will be surprised how quickly you rush to the page *to resolve Monday's crisis*. Starting your day by solving yesterday's problem will have excited you enough to move the characters down *into the next valley and up to the next peak*. As you reach the top, stop.

Feed your dog. Make a payment on your car. Answer a want ad.

On Wednesday, alive with curiosity, you will deftly resolve the crisis in which your heroes will have placed themselves on Tuesday.

And so on. And steadily, always steadily.

Your characters will cry to you to HELP.

Do not listen.

Tell them you've had a busy day, and you want to spend the afternoon doing a crossword puzzle or writing your congressman.

So much of writing is knowing when not to write, of knowing precisely when to stop.

I must add that by "crisis" I am not necessarily implying that every two pages is another segment of *The Perils of Pauline,* that every moment of the text is an outrageous cliffhanger. The crisis may be nothing more than the introduction of a mysterious but pivotal character. As soon as she enters, and you feel a rush of excitement in your stomach, *stop*.

Force may be defined as not only the enthusiasms of your will, but also as the deliberate and sustained titillation of the author by his or her own characters.

The *force* of writing not only is a physical act, but also a psychological, if not psychic one. The wells of creativity all too easily can be exhausted by excessive thirst. But moderate, steady drinking keeps the well at a plentiful level. Implied in this example is the assumption that the more balanced and moderate your pace, the steadier your writing.

Both Norman Mailer and Ernest Hemingway have stated that each time they began a novel they had to behave as if they were in training for a fight. Personally, while admiring the impulse behind the metaphor, I prefer *coitus interruptus*, if only because I've been in one fight in my life, found it embarrassing for all concerned, and much prefer grappling with love.

Following this sexy plan of mine, your enthusiasm for the work, your excitement and involvement in the lives of the characters will be sustained for the length of time necessary to accomplish its creation. Moreover if you are working towards a deadline, you will know exactly how long the writing will take to achieve. (Scene 1 to 1st crisis, 1 day; resolution of 1st crisis: introduction of Madame Mystery, 2nd day, etc.).

Most of all, you will be able to write seven days a week and not feel like Mailer after his match with Hemingway.

You will keep alive the *immediacy*, the present tense of your work.

Being stimulated to know what happens next, your excitement will generate the characters' own excitement. Hopefully, *his* or *her* enthusiasm will be conveyed to the reader or audience.

The *force* of the characters and of their lives is sufficient to fill a blank page, the mirror of your own imaginings, the restlessness of hidden realities prodded into being.

The enthusiasm for the growing events sustains your force.

Each day resolves a crisis, then creates another as inner lives unfold.

Force and form.

What is needed to complete the magical operation, the principal aspect of the trine without which nothing is realized?

Idea.
But first a word about ghosts.

Many writers see them. They give them names: Perhaps they call them Dostoevski, Buñuel, Hemingway, Fellini, Strindberg, or even John Simon.

These ghosts are conjured up by the writers' own fears of failure. Ghosts feed on this fear. They stand over the writers' shoulder, leering and intoning, "I would have done it differently, moron. I never would have written it *that* way."

To banish the ghosts, who are nothing but smoky, self-created vampires, the writer must realize that it is *his or her job alone* to discover the world of character—and not Dostoevski's, Buñuel's, Fellini's, or even John Simon's job. Dostoevski himself may have had a ghost called Pushkin; or Fellini, Rossellini. But eventually Dostoevski wrote *Crime and Punishment*, and Fellini made 8½.

As soon as the creator realized that *nobody else was entitled to define that specific inner world*, composed of heart, soul, and mind (another mysterious trine), the ghosts vanished.

Muses are something else.

At the very least, an invocation to your favorite genius may give you a rosy glow which may well turn into a volcanic force.

Support your personal *genius loci*, or Guardian Angel, if you will—but leave the ghosts alone.

Idea

You understand the formal aspect of the screenplay.
You possess the will and force to see the work to its conclusion.

But what are your dramatic concerns?

Whatever they are, they should be prompted by your deepest enthusiasms, nightmares, obsessions, interests, lyric pulse.

Let us assume the concerns spring from character.

Then the toss and turn of your characters' life will generate the Idea of your work.

The tumbling will create an audience.

For example, *Citizen Kane* presents us with a variety of ideas: the power of the press; the art of propaganda; childhood as the major psychological influence in man's development.

But when Leland visits Kane and says "You talk about the people as though they belong to you," we are certain that the writer's basic concerns are with *creating a larger-than-life character*. For all the cinematic pyrotechnics, and Welles' wondrous theatricality, *we remember Kane himself*.

Implied in this statement of intent is the notion that character *is* idea. This is a debatable point, needless to say. Certainly an idea may generate characters which are but necessary pawns to give flesh to that idea or ideas.

And yet in dramatic literature, characters seem to generate ideas, rather than the reverse.

The richer the characterization, the greater the wealth of ideas implied.

In *On the Waterfront* Terry Malloy's despair tells us a great deal about the realities of more than boxing and the waterfront itself: "See! You don't understand! I could've been a contender. I could've had class and been somebody. Real class. Instead of a bum." He embodies *everybody's* spurned hopes.

When I first began to write, I read a text by a Hungarian named Lajos Egri. It was called *The Art of Dramatic Writing*. In his work Egri managed to reduce the creative act to a nearly mathematical formula. Every piece of writing began with the question: *What is my theme?* Interestingly enough, Egri managed to turn Shakespeare into an instant philosopher. Principally Shakespeare was a lover of drama, and therefore of character. But theatrical technique and character, according to Egri, merely served to clothe a philosophical skeleton.

For several weeks, while I struggled with Egri's book, I began to wonder if ever I would write at all. Perhaps I would do better sitting with Sartre at the Deux Magots, or listening to Egri himself hold forth at the Hotel Gellert in Budapest.

Fortunately I fell in love, and the feeling was so awkward that I began to write a short story about falling in love, and about awkwardness in falling in love, and that for me was the end of Lajos Egri.

A dream, a memory, the brush of a sleeve against your cheek, the end of the world . . . Let it implode within your psyche. Close your eyes and wait until it begins to gather shape, and a figure emerges.

Idea + Force + Form = Idea Realized.

Earlier in the text I had written that it is important to know when to *stop* writing.

It is equally important to know when to *start:*
When?
When the figures emerge in your mind's eye.
When you sense a human pulse beyond your own.
This is not metaphysical musing but practical advice.
Often you might begin a work when the character is merely half-formed, or the idea not fully conceived.

Start when you see the characters, hear them, sense their separateness from your own identity. Then you may begin to race towards them. But *not before* this sensation begins.

Strangely, you will find you are dealing with a different kind of intelligence in this procedure, a sense that is purely intuitive. Ultimately you will have to learn to trust your intuition, which is a balance of the wisdom of your being and the knowledge you have learned. And perhaps something even more. (The Muses? Your *genius loci*?)

It is your intuition which will tell you when to begin to write.

To learn how to trust the most profound part of yourself is the basis of the act of writing. Of creating anything.

All else becomes irrelevant.

And lest you think I have begun to soar to arcane realms, prepare yourselves for a landing.

We are going to discuss certain aspects of the language of film.

About the Camera

"I found myself one late afternoon standing at the edge of a mist-enshrouded street. It was impossible to judge the width or length of this place, for the fog had begun to capture the cracks and avenues of the city several hours before my arrival. I could not say whether such misty abundance was a natural or unnatural phenomenon in this spot, due to the time of day, season, or year, for it was my first trip to this part of the world.

A thin and yellow streetlamp was the only source of illumination. Perhaps the bulb was damp, or the wiring faulty, for the lamp kept sparking, humming, spitting.

Soon the fog grew thicker.

Slowly, with an arm before me, I began to move towards what I thought to be the end of the lane, and to where the map had defined the river. My hand brushed against a damp wall. I turned, began to move forward, then bruised my knuckles on another wall. My hand came away, stickily, from its surface. I turned once more. Another wall. Yet another."

From *The Adventures of Lajos Egri*,
by Stephen Geller

How to translate this imaginary scene into film? Describe:

1. The Setting and Time of Day;
2. The Characters and Dramatic Action;
3. The Dialogue (if the scene requires it);
4. Only those SHOTS necessary for the *telling of the story*.

The first step is easy:

1 — EXT. LANE — LATE AFTERNOON   1

The second step becomes a bit more complicated. The simple declarative sentences you would use to describe the Character and the Action should resemble the *feeling* of the text, or its idea. Also they should convey the rhythm of the scene. The rhythm, in this case, will be determined by the movement of the camera.

First let us talk about the feeling or tone of the text.

There is an obvious contrast between the dry, almost pseudo-rational narration of events, and the dreamlike quality of the setting. We want to convey a sense of reason becoming slowly shrouded in fog. Therefore we will want the camera to describe the interaction between the man, the objects on the lane, and fog which eventually covers both.

The rhythm of the scene will be slow and mysterious.

1—EXT. LANE—LATE AFTERNOON   1
ESTABLISHING SHOT of a mist-enshrouded lane: two undefined walls on either side of the FRAME (a garden? building?) which disappear into the mist. A yellow streetlamp giving small and fitful light. Then THE SOUND OF FOOTSTEPS approaching slowly, stopping.
ANGLE of EGRI, standing at the edge of the lane. He is wearing a trenchcoat, hat, and muffler, and carries a suitcase. Middle-aged, anonymous-looking, EGRI stares about him. FROM HIS POV WE SEE: the lane disappearing into a fog which has begun to grow thicker. SOUND of the streetlamp sputtering, flickering in the mist. SOUND of the dripping of fog against pavement.

EGRI pulls a map from his pocket, and brings it up to his face, squinting. TIGHT OF THE MAP: an area has been circled in red, but the language in which it is written is incomprehensible. With his finger, EGRI follows a line on the map. SLOWLY THE CAMERA LIFTS TO THE MAN'S FACE: he is thoroughly confused.

        EGRI (*Almost a whisper*)
River?

EGRI picks up the suitcase and begins to move forward through the fog, holding an outstretched hand before him. THE SCREEN seems to swirl in mist, EGRI becoming a mere outline. THE SOUND of the crackling of the streetlamp. Suddenly EGRI'S hand snaps back. He frowns. Pats the space before him, slowly. Discovers he has walked into a wall.

   Bloody damn.

EGRI turns, holding out his hand again. He takes two steps forward, then stops. TIGHT OF HIS EYES: tearing, smarting.

   What?

He looks down, brings his hand up to his face. His knuckles are bleeding. He whips about.
CAMERA PULLS UP SLOWLY IN AERIAL DOLLY TO REVEAL EGRI enclosed within four walls, and looking around him in a panic.
The mists roll in. He becomes a shadow.
               DISSOLVE TO:

2—INT. GELLER'S STUDY—EVENING
TIGHT of a brandy snifter being warmed between two hands.

THE SCENE contains:
1. AN ESTABLISHING SHOT, which introduces the setting.

2. SOUND EFFECTS.
3. AN ANGLE that is nonspecific, and which allows the director to shoot from a position of his choice. (In the reading of the script, however, ANGLE OF immediately implies a different and a stranger cut, *a break in the rhythm* of the scene.)
4. A SHOT FROM THE MAN'S POINT-OF-VIEW (POV) which lets his eyes become our own.
5. A TIGHT SHOT of the map (also from EGRI'S POV). TIGHT is another word for CLOSE-UP. Either word can be used.
6. An implied REVERSE ANGLE, where the CAMERA LIFTS TO THE MAN'S face.
7. The implied movement of the CAMERA behind EGRI as he crosses through the fog.
8. CAMERA PULLING UP SLOWLY IN AERIAL DOLLY TO REVEAL another establishing shot, a slowly lifting bird's-eye view of EGRI within walls.
9. The image DISSOLVING from Scene 1 to Scene 2; that is, the last image of the panicky, shadowy man dissolving into the first image of the next scene, a brandy snifter held between two hands.

Wow.

I can write a list of the shots and angles used in screenwriting, and I will.

But how do you know which ones to use?

The easiest thing to do is *close your eyes, set up an imaginary screen in your inner forehead, and play the scene*.

Whisper to yourself: I see a lane, hear the sound of a man approaching, etc.

Try to visualize the exact scene.

You will be surprised how *easily* you do this.

Since your birth you've been conditioned by films and (heaven help you) television to think of much in images. For better or for worse, the language of much of this century has been a language of imagery. In all likelihood, you are writing a screenplay because, unconsciously, you already have seen your story and characters.

Now begin to dream-screen the scene.

How would the playing of the scene excite you?

What images would stimulate you?

I rather like the above work.

I'm curious about Egri.

I seem to be in a territory occupied by Buñuel, Graham Greene, Carol Reed. . . . What atmosphere, splendid shots, odd visual tension.

"And such marvelous business, the man enclosed in the walls, and seemingly trapped in a brandy snifter, I mean the *cutting* is absolutely superb!"

"Hats off to the director and the editor!"

Maybe so.

I would also say hats off to *me*, since I just wrote the scene myself, and told the director exactly what I wanted, and gave him character, atmosphere, event, and a sublime piece of cutting that will earn him a line in the *New York Times* as being ingenious or, to be sniffy and superior, clever.

Another rule (oh they keep creeping in):

When in doubt, dream the scene.

When not in doubt, *dream the scene anyway.*

Remember, *your character will give you clues to the universe you are creating.*

No matter how conditioned you have been by other films, images, television brutality, if you listen to your characters' voices, if you follow their dilemma, they will lead you into their own universe, and will help you *direct the scene* as you consciously dream it.

They will show you, by their movements, exactly where to put and how to use the camera.

Then you will take pen, pencil, typewriter or word processor, and *write what you just have witnessed.*

If you are stuck for terms, you may consult the following list, and see if any of the shots fit *what your character has shown you;* if not, invent them.

Camera Angles and Cutting Techniques

---

1. The Four Basic Camera Shots

1. ESTABLISHING SHOT

   A complete view of the setting in which the scene is to occur.

2. TIGHT SHOT, OR CLOSE-UP (C.U.)

   As close a shot as possible of a person or an object: this is used as an exclamation point within the scene.

3. MEDIUM SHOT

   Generally a shot of a person or a group in which only a partial aspect of the person or group is revealed.

4. LONG SHOT

   An angle of a group or place seen from a distance.

2. Camera Movement

1. CAMERA PANS TO

   A panoramic shot, in which the camera moves from one horizontal point to another. Generally the shot is used either as an establishing shot, linking one action to another, or as the point-of-view of one character or narrator surveying a scene or event.

2. CAMERA TILTS UP

   The camera, generally in a medium or tight

shot, moves up vertically from one part of an object or person, to another part.

3. CAMERA ZOOMS TO

   A shot racing towards an object a great distance away. Aesthetically it is one of the most unnatural and bizarre shots in film, and should be used sparingly. Because of the extremity of its focal length, all background appears flat and wiped-out.

4. CAMERA TRACKS (OR DOLLIES) TO

   The camera, either mounted on tracks, or on a carriage which moves electrically, is pushed into a scene. Generally, the shot is used as if the camera were a character, moving into an event.

5. CAMERA PULLS BACK TO REVEAL

   The shot begins tight upon an object, and then pulls away from the object, revealing the rest of the setting, or a good part of it. This is another exclamation point.

6. FROM (CHARACTER'S) POV, or POINT-OF-VIEW

   The action is shot as if one camera were a character's eyes. This is tricky, and must be used sparingly. A scene shot from the POV of more than one person is confusing to the viewer, and a nightmare to the editor. (It would be the equivalent of writing a paragraph in which each sentence is cowritten from the POV of a different character.)

7. AERIAL DOLLY (OR CRANE) SHOT OF

   An overhead shot, taken from a crane, of the action. If the scene is in movement (as in our example) you should specify AERIAL UP (starting from the ground) or AERIAL DOWN (moving to the ground).

End of Scene

1)   FADE OUT:

FADE IN:

The last image of Scene A fades to black, and the first image of Screen B fades in.

2)   DISSOLVE TO:

The last image of Scene A starts to fade. *Midway through the fade* the first image of Scene B fades in.

3/4)   CUT TO:

As I stated earlier, this is rarely used, since the cut between Scene A and the beginning of Scene B is implied. If you feel the end of the scene needs a strong punctuation, write

                                          QUICK CUT TO:

This will alert the director or editor that the last image or line of Scene A demands a strong finish, therefore, a sharp cut.

5)   CROSSCUT TO:

If two scenes are going to occur simultaneously in two different places (Scene A, Scene B, Scene A, Scene B), then CROSSCUT TO generally is used. It will be obvious to the careful reader that the dramatic situation is ABAB, but writing CROSSCUT TO makes the situation more apparent to the reader.

Note that, with the exception of FADE IN, written on the left-hand margin of the page, all the other end-of-scene instructions are written on the right-hand margin.

A Few Other Effects

1. *Split-screen*
To the left, Scene A; to the right, Scene B.

Rarely is the split-screen used. Even more rarely, when it *is* used, is it used *well*. The split-screen is a screen divided in half, where two different scenes are playing simultaneously. Unless the action on both screens is so well-defined, and both actions dramatically related to each other, the effect is confusing.

Split-screen is so dramatic that it calls attention to itself.

More often than not the audience falls away from the dream.

2. *Montage*
A montage is a series of short images which collectively grow in rhythm and intensity to complete a full dramatic event or statement.

The easiest way to delineate a montage in a screenplay is to write, for example:

```
1— (DRAMATIC EVENT) MONTAGE                    1
     A. ANGLE OF X, then brief description.
     B. SHOT OF B. Description.
     C. TIGHT OF C. No description needed.
               Et cetera.
```

In effect, you are outlining a complete sequence with specific aspects of action, character, and objects delineated for the director. If you wish you may even describe how slowly or quickly you wish the montage to be cut. Most often a montage is without dialogue. (The classic textbook example of a great montage is Eisenstein's "Steps of Petersburg" sequence, from *Potemkin*.)

Geller's oft-repeated words of advice:

Use only those CAMERA ANGLES and rhythmic devices that are necessary to the storytelling.

The above list is a basic grammar, and for the time, is all you need know.

The simplest way to tell the story is to dream it on your mind-screen.

If at first you find yourself forcing the CAMERA to move a certain way, stop.

Write the event of the scene as if it were a short story, forgetting that the camera even exists. Later, when you revise the work, try to imagine the scene in formal screenplay terms. (I see the eyes of a woman: TIGHT OF WOMAN'S EYES.) It is not a difficult exercise. After a while, it becomes automatic.

Do not worry about the camera terms. With practice, you will become familiar with them.

Your greatest contribution is *not* a knowledge of camera techniques, but the ability to create characters and to tell a story. Where you place the camera, and how you move it completely will depend upon the reality of the characters themselves, and what you will want the audience to feel and to know about them. Remember: even a chimpanzee can move a camera.

But can he tap-dance a tale?

Thus far I have concerned myself with *your* relationship to the characters, and therefore to the idea of the screenplay. From this, ostensibly, your enthusiasm for such contact will provide you with the force to follow your characters in the screenplay form.

This inner recognition, however, is merely one half of the creative process.

The other half of the process is the *external presentation of materials*.

Simply, you've dreamed it up.

Now dream it down.

What is the best way to dramatize your characters to the reader or audience? Your personal relationship to the characters, after all, must be understood fully before you can begin to maneuver them before the public.

Bear in mind that nothing in this procedure is as clear-cut as I have written.

For example, you may think you understand your characters perfectly well, then find that during the revisions you might have ignored a startlingly obvious detail; or perhaps you've discovered a novel event which now seems to give one character a different face. In that case, your structure automatically will change.

Since your mental and emotional living room now is filled with newfound friends, you had best deal with this turn of events as you would in the equivalent physical situation: make sure everyone is comfortable, all the while being aware that this fine party might well turn into a rout. Deal with the situation patiently, with tact and humor.

Each time I begin a new piece of work, I am emphatically aware of this process.

It could be said that I am grim with emphasis.

And yet, in my enthusiasm and excitement, nearly every time I forget it.

Somewhere after the rough draft I find myself having to review the inner realities of the characters themselves.

To some extent I can excuse myself because my oversight was due to the novelty of seeing stretches of new territory appear before me, and rushing blindly down the dune or into the forest. (Do not be confused. Simply because I am writing a book, this does not give me the status of an expert; probably I have more in common with Egri than I would wish to admit.)

To recapitulate: the process of dreaming and thinking presents you with characters and themes.

Giving yourself time to play well with these characters allows you to know them well. Once you think and feel you know who they are, the process of writing allows you to present them to the public or reader.

It is a twofold task, with each aspect (dreaming, presenting) both reinforcing and, at times (regrettably), undermining the other.

Patience, humor, goodwill towards your characters and yourself will help you to achieve what is a mysterious process: *to make tangible the intangible; to produce something from nothing*.

Let us assume you've mastered the first part of our magical equation, *idea + force + form*. How do you combine these elements to produce the answer, the *realized idea*?

Part Two, while not permanently solving the equation, will point to several methods which might well lead you to a solution.

Part Two:
Idea Realized

Methods of Storytelling

All of us know how to read.

Some of us assert we even read *well*.

Those of us who write consider ourselves skilled in the art of reading.

But how many of us, *soi-disant* amateurs or professionals alike, actually examine a text not only for the effects of the event or characterizations, the resonance of the author's language or imagery, *but also for the physical construction itself*? The method by which the author makes us focus upon his left hand while his right is engaged in tricky business?

How many of us have seen a film, read a novel, play or screenplay from the inside out, as it were, asking ourselves: *what did the author want us to experience at this moment? how did he elicit that response*?

In Part Two, therefore, we will study certain techniques of craft: exposition, character, and narrative development, dialogue, rhythm, and resolution.

Whether you write dramatic plays, screen comedies or novels, eventually you will find yourself asking *how best can I convey my characters or dramatic situation to an audience*?

Obviously if you are writing exclusively for yourself, then you've already solved this problem, have wasted good money purchasing this book, and minutes getting this far into the text; more, if you are considering improv-

ing upon Godard, the *nouveau roman*, or believe there is
no difference between fiction and nonfiction, then this
work is a thoroughly reactionary tract, and I a villainous
scumbag of Victorian notions.

Victorian, nothing.

I am going to be ragingly Elizabethan, if not in spirit,
at least in example.

Most of the how-to's you will encounter in the following pages are taken from the works of the finest dramatist
in the English language.

Do not be shocked.

Yes, this book still is about the process of screenwriting.

But Elizabethan stagecraft more closely resembles
film technique—in short scenes, quick cutting, setting
shift, imagery to show internal states, breadth of characterization—than does modern theater.

And *all of it* is dramatic literature.

There will be a few examples from film, scattered
herein. But there is *no* writer of comedy and drama
greater than Shakespeare, no other writer who has left us
so rich a treasury of experiments in craft, as well as . . . all
the rest. (You know. Poetry. Language. That sort of thing.)

There have been as many books and articles written
about "that sort of thing" as there have been productions
of Shakespeare's plays. But few books have dealt with the
question of "How-He-Did-It-That-We-May-Do-It-Too."

Let us examine elements of dramatic writing, therefore,
with examples culled from the works of that eminently
engaging Elizabethan. At the very least, by the time
you've finished this second part, you will have discovered
a new way of asking questions about craft, as well as
appreciating how the greatest master craftsman of the
stage solved a problem or two.

But before we begin, let me show you an important
bit of legerdemain.

The First Ten Minutes Are Crucial

Here's a wonderful rule to try to break: The first ten minutes of film are the most crucial ones.

Why?

Because in the first ten minutes *the audience is going to accept any and all conventions of your universe, provided that you do not decide to alter these conventions midway through work*.

Here are two examples of the remarks of a disgruntled public when confronted with a broken agreement:

1. Response to convention broken *midway through the film*. "What? But I thought we were in Africa! You mean, all along the story took place in that woman's cellar?"
2. Response to convention broken *at the end of the film*. "Insane! Do you mean that man who gave the knife to the Constable was actually King Lear? What are we asked to believe next?"

What, indeed.

Consider the difference, however, when those bits of information and establishment of character are utilized *at the beginning of the film*. No matter how patently bizarre or ridiculous the situation may seem, an audience will be prepared to accept it at the story's outset—if for no other reason than the fact that they've paid their money, and, thus, have entered into an agreement with the author to be entertained.

At the *opening of the film,* therefore:

1) If Miss Princebottle takes young Gerald to her

cellar, removes a small Edwardian compact from her bodice and whispers, "Gaze deeply, Gerald, into this mirror. Do you not see a curious ape?" Gerald tears himself away from Miss Princebottle's bodice, and gazes. *Presto*, we are in Africa, and Gerald is confronted with a drooling ape.

Equally *presto*! the audience will accept this unconventional bit of space travel, since the author has stated in dramatic terms the physical conventions of the film. (Bodice to mirror to travel. A magical Princebottle.)

2) An old man stands upon a bleak moor, holding a bloody knife. A crown sits askew upon the fellow's head. OFF-CAMERA WE HEAR THE VOICE OF CONSTABLE CREWS: "Sorry, sir, we can't go struttin' about the moors, can we, wearin' crowns and carryin' daggers." The CONSTABLE enters the FRAME as the OLD MAN turns to him, with pathetic traces of authority. "Here, let me take that knife from you, sir, bring you back to the village. You could do with a bit of soup, I'd imagine. What's your name?" Cocking an eyebrow, the OLD MAN intones, "King Lear."

Do we laugh? Cry? Giggle nervously?

We continue to sit in our seats *to see what happens*.

The initial ten minutes of playing time is best used *to define the conventions of your drama: to set the tone* of the piece as you introduce character and event. Through manipulation of mood, voice, and atmosphere, the first ten minutes clues the audience to the physical and psychic reality of your universe.

The audience will accept anything at this point, because they still are filled with the expectations of an evening.

This opening gambit is one of the subtler tricks of *exposition*.

A few more examples:

Think of the opening sequence of Fellini's 8½.

GUIDO, the protagonist, is caught in a tunnel in a traffic jam. Soon he is being poisoned by auto fumes. He cannot leave his car. He begins to kick at the window. All around him stare disinterestedly.

He manages to climb through the window.

He soars into the sky.

Then he is being flown like a kite, by his LAWYER and PRODUCTION MANAGER. He cannot escape, and plunges into the ocean.

WE ARE in his bedroom as he awakens from this nightmare. A DOCTOR examines him. GUIDO is suffering from fatigue.

In these three sequences, GUIDO'S DREAM and his AWAKENING, we have learned a great deal about Fellini's protagonist: he is under intense physical and psychological pressure; he is trying to escape that pressure, but is unable. He is trapped.

We have also learned that the film-maker will enter Guido's mind, and *so the movie will leap from physical reality to Guido's dreams and fantasies*.

As an audience, therefore, we will have accepted the leaping of the film, the cutting between fantasy and reality.

Another example:

In the first eighty seconds of Bob Fosse's *All That Jazz*, we hear, over a black screen, a voice give a musical countdown. Then we see a Broadway sign reading *All That Jazz*. Then, over a black screen again, we hear terrible coughing, then strains of Vivaldi playing over a quick montage of the protagonist, Joe Gideon, turning up the tape of the music, putting drops into his eyes, taking a shower (with cigarette in mouth), downing dexadrines and staring at himself in the mirror: "It's showtime, folks!" he says. Immediately JOE is on a high-wire, doing a terrible balancing act. His comely Death Muse admires his living on the edge, then watches him plummet sixty feet to a safety net.

In those eighty seconds, Fosse has told us a great deal about his protagonist, the tempo and turns of his life: daring, a fatalist, hopped-up, jazzy.

Even more, he has set the form of the film: a rapid, gunshot montage which mirrors Gideon's life, thoughts, fantasies.

In both examples, as the psychological state of the

characters has been dramatized, so, too, have the *physical conventions of the film:* the movement from fantasy to reality, from projection and dream to externals pressures.

There is another basic rule implied in these examples. In all instances, the stories are SHOWN, *not* TOLD. *All are dramatized. All move forward, whether inward, outward or upward.*

Let us look at the examples of Lear and Miss Princebottle once again.

Neither scene relies upon a lengthy monologue by an old man ("What am I, an old man, doing here, on this moor?") or by Miss Princebottle ("Now see here, Gerald: I think you're going to find this amusing: soon we will go to my cellar where I will remove a mirror from my bodice. Once this occurs, you are to stare into the depths." And so on.).

Show characters and action. *Don't* talk about them.

Show their emotional state. *Don't* let them tell you about it.

In the first ten minutes of playing time, introduce the terms of your world THROUGH GESTURE and ACTION.

Now let us tiptoe up the aisle, leaving Miss Princebottle with her young charge, Lear with the Constable, and see how Shakespeare himself has used *his* opening gambit in *Macbeth.*

Elements of Exposition

Exposition is the art of showing the members of the audience exactly what the author wants them to see of character second event.

As you read the following examples of exposition,

pretend you are in a theater, and witnessing the event for the first time.

Ask yourself:

1. *What does the author want me to know?*
2. *What does he want me to feel?*

Once you've answered these questions, then ask yourself:

3. *How does he accomplish this?*

I,i
[*Thunder and lightning. Enter THREE WITCHES.*]

1st WITCH	When shall we three meet again, In thunder, lightning, or in rain?
2nd WITCH	When the hurlyburly's done, When the battle's lost and won.
3rd WITCH	That will be ere the set of sun.
1st WITCH	Where the place?
2nd WITCH	Upon the heath.
3rd WITCH	There to meet with Macbeth.
1st WITCH	I come, Graymalkin!
2nd WITCH	Paddock calls.
3rd WITCH	Anon!
ALL	Fair is foul, and foul is fair. Hover through the fog and filthy air. [*Exeunt.*]

In a mere eleven lines of dialogue, how does Shakespeare utilize exposition? What, in fact, are the elements of exposition?

1. Setting
The geography of the drama seems to be blasted, foul, supernatural. Nothing (and perhaps nobody) is what it seems.

2. Atmosphere
A universe of dread ambiguity is implied in "Fair is foul, and foul is fair." Tension and suspense "hover through the fog and filthy air."

3. Introduction of Characters
Three witches appear, dramatized as capable of creating storms in nature ("When shall we three meet again/in thunder, lightning, or in rain?"), and perhaps in man. Moreover, the witches show themselves to be capable of prophecy. ("That will be ere the set of sun.") In this opening gambit, they seem to be cast as powerful agents of abnormal, malignant change, able to make man's state dependent upon his hideous, supernatural surroundings.

4. Action
The scene begins *at the end of a scene*. (How's that for bravura stagecraft?) Three witches have set in motion an action in which someone named Macbeth will be involved. They agree to meet before sunset, at the conclusion of a battle, on the heath, and in an atmospheric condition they themselves will create.

5. Language
Chanted, ritualistic. Each witch speaks three times, then all speak as a choral force. The first witch asks a question, the other two reply. All three quickly respond to their familiar spirits calling, then act as a practicing witch chorus, setting the moral order of the world on its tail with "Fair is foul, and foul is fair."

It is the end of the first magical operation, the chant a summation of their will, and the beginning of the next beat.

6. Rhythm of Scene
Thunder and lightning. Emptiness.

Three witches appear, charged with the performance of a nasty operation. They agree to meet with Macbeth, then ensure the solidity of their performance by the incantation of "Fair is foul." The exit, perhaps to the roll of thunder, following.

7. Theme

"Fair is foul, and foul is fair" rings in our ears, carrying over into the next scene.

Even before this hopeless and paradoxical condition is related, the witches allude to a battle both "lost and won," so the puzzle of the drama already has begun. The universe of the play is going to be riddled with events and people whose facade continually shifts before our eyes, or so the author implies.

In *eleven lines*, Shakespeare has presented the possibilities of a topsy-turvy world, where nature and supernature contend for domination.

Exposition uses the elements of setting, atmosphere, rhythm, and language to introduce both character and event.

It also may well hint at a theme.

Note how Shakespeare creates *the feeling of anticipation* in the audience by alluding to a magical act performed before the curtain rises ("When shall we three meet again?") and a future confrontation between the weird sisters and a certain Macbeth.

Immediately we want to know what will happen.

Who is Macbeth? Why is he important to these witches?

What will be his role in their drama?

What, in fact, *is* the drama?

Nothing, after all, actually *happens* in this scene. But, by placing us between two events, and in a state of atmospheric tension, Shakespeare has created a sense of immense expectation, of nervous curiosity in the audience.

In eleven lines, the stage is set, the moral order dreadfully intoned.

And all of it occurred *in less than one minute*.

This is a rare and stunning example of a Muse kissing an author on the brow.

Let us see, in the following scene, how Shakespeare *answers the questions he has raised* about Macbeth and the witches.

I,ii

[*Alarum within. Enter* KING DUNCAN, MALCOLM, DONALBAIN, LENNOX, *with attendants, meeting a bleeding* CAPTAIN.]

KING
> What bloody man is that? He can report, —
> As 'seemeth by his plight, of the revolt
> The newest state.

MALCOLM   This is the sergeant
> Who like a good and hardy soldier fought
> 'Gainst my captivity. Hail, brave friend!
> Say to the King the knowledge of the broil
> As thou didst leave it.

> Is this the battle both lost and won? Who is
> Macbeth? The Captain tells us.

CAPTAIN   Doubtful it stood,
> As two spent swimmers that do cling together
> And choke their art. The merciless Macdonwald
> (Worthy to be a rebel, for to that
> The multiplying villanies of nature
> Do swarm upon him) from the Western Isles
> Of kerns and gallowglasses is supplied;
> And Fortune, on his damned quarrel smiling,
> Showed like a rebel's whore. But all's too weak:
> For Brave Macbeth (well he deserves that name),
> Disdaining Fortune, with his brandished steel,
> Which smoked with bloody execution,
> Like valor's minion carved out his passage
> Till he faced the slave;
> Which ne'er shook hands nor bade farewell to
>   him
> Till he unseamed him from the nave to th' chops
> And fixed his head upon our battlements.

KING
> O valiant cousin! worthy gentleman!

In the first scene we had heard of a battle, and know that Macbeth somehow is involved. Now, in the above lines, more is revealed concerning both the battle and Macbeth. (Note that each scene *slowly but specifically reveals one aspect of character and action.* It is as if the author were playing us as fish, giving us just enough line to lure us further towards the hook.)

1. Narrative Event
A revolt has occurred in the north of Scotland, led by a Norwegian king and aided by Irish rebels. The outcome appears doubtful until Macbeth plunges into battle and, with stunning ferocity, begins to carve up the rebels.

2. Character Revelation
Macbeth is depicted by the Captain as a brave warrior; by the King as a valiant cousin, a worthy gentleman; in short, a man of heroic proportions. (What, we ask, do the witches want of such a man?)

3. Setting
After the wretchedness of the moors, the solidity of Duncan's castle, the substantial weight of court life appears a veritable refuge. The alarm sounded, the entrance of the King and his court give us the sense that man's state may be more permanent than the witches plan.

4. Tone
And yet this momentary sense of stability is shattered by the appearance of a *bleeding* captain. His description of men in battle, and especially of Macbeth's bloodthirstiness cannot but make us feel *something* is amiss; more, in the very solid and seemingly eternal monument of a castle we hear of a revolt. Is "Fair is foul" already at work?

But let us continue.

CAPTAIN
  As whence the sun 'gins his reflection
  Shipwracking storms and direful thunders break,
  So from that spring whence comfort seemed to come,
  Discomfort swells. Mark, King of Scotland, mark.
  No sooner justice had, with valor armed,
  Compelled these skipping kerns to trust their heels

> But the Norweyan lord, surveying vantage,
> With furbished arms and new supplies of men,
> Began a fresh assault.

KING   Dismayed not this
> Our captains, Macbeth and Banquo?

CAPTAIN   Yes,
> As sparrows eagles, or the hare the lion.
> If I say sooth, I must report they were
> As cannons overcharged with double cracks,
> So they doubly redoubled strokes upon the foe.
> Except they meant to bathe in reeking wounds,
> Or memorize another Golgotha,
> I cannot tell—
> But I am faint; my gashes cry for help.

KING
> So well thy words become thee as thy wounds,
> They smack of honor both. Go get him surgeons.
>   [*Exit* CAPTAIN, *attended*.]
>   [*Enter* ROSS *and* ANGUS.]
> Who comes here?

MALCOLM   The worthy Thane of Ross.

LENNOX
> What a haste looks through his eyes! So should
> He look that seems to speak things strange.

ROSS   God save the King!

KING
> Whence cam'st thou, worthy Thane?

ROSS   From Fife, great King,
> Where the Norweyan banners flout the sky
> And fan our people cold.
> Norway himself, with terrible numbers,
> Assisted by that most disloyal traitor
> The Thane of Cawdor, began a dismal conflict,
> Till that Bellona's bridegroom, lapped in proof,
> Confronted him with self-comparisons
> Point against point rebellious, arm 'gainst arm,
> Curbing his lavish spirit: and to conclude,
> The victory fell on us.

KING   Great happiness!

ROSS   That now

Sweno, the Norways' king, craves composition;
Nor would we deign him burial of his men
Till he disbursed, at Saint Colme's Inch,
Ten thousand dollars to our general use.

KING

No more that Thane of Cawdor shall deceive
Our bosom interest. Go pronounce his present death
And with his former title greet Macbeth.

ROSS

I'll see it done.

KING

What he hath lost noble Macbeth hath won.

1. Narrative Event

The battle turns in favor of the Norwegians. The captain, horribly wounded, cannot describe the outcome. In a near faint, he is led offstage to the surgeons. The first part of this two-part scene is concluded.

The second part begins with the entrance of the Lords Ross and Angus, who report that the Thane of Cawdor turned traitor, throwing his support to the Norwegians. And yet, although the Norwegians' attack was furious, it was repulsed, and the victory fell to Duncan. Now the Norwegians wish to surrender. The King dispatches Ross to pronounce the death sentence upon Cawdor, and to give Macbeth his title.

2. Characterization

Duncan, first of all, is seen to be a just ruler, distributing favor where it merits, and death when it is required.

The captain is a neatly stroked character, presented by Shakespeare in a vivid, somewhat shell-shocked fashion. His irony ("Yes, as sparrows eagles, or the hare the lion") is no courtier's tool. Duncan's response to his speech is compassionate and authoritative.

Macbeth still has not made an appearance, *and yet his name has been mentioned five times in two scenes* and, in the latter, characterized by the Captain as *brave*, and by Duncan as *valiant*, *worthy*, and *honored* as the new Thane of Cawdor.

3. Tone

The contrast between two characters (The Captain's vivid, rough speech, and Duncan's eloquence) is well depicted here. Moreover, Duncan's reaction to the Captain's speech infers a great deal about his own character: Macbeth, so it would seem, is worthy to serve such a king.

4. The Division of the Scenes

By dividing the action of the second scene into two parts (King, Captain; King, Ross), Shakespeare gives us a sense of timely, *urgent acceleration*. A great deal is happening even as they speak. The action is so swift, in fact, that even while the Captain is describing one aspect of the battle, Ross is on his way to narrate its resolution. The end of the scene seems to contradict the "Fair is foul" loss of order among men.

5. Language

Note the rhyming couplets throughout the witches' scene.

They are nasty, childlike, direct; literally spellbinding.

Shakespeare then shifts, in the second scene, to iambic pentameter, the "royal roll' of the voice. The contrast between the language in both scenes is deafeningly effective. Shakespeare caps the end of the second scene with an arhythmic, nonmetrical couplet:

ROSS
    I'll see it done.
KING
    What he hath lost noble Macbeth hath won.

This serves as an exclamation point, stressing "noble Macbeth" in our consciousness. And yet, by virtue of the quality of the rhyme, it perhaps unconsciously recalls the witches' own language.

We still have not met Macbeth.

We still do not know what the witches require of him.

At this point all we know is that Macbeth is a great captain, will soon be made Thane of Cawdor; is a loyal and worthy subject of Duncan's.

Order, it would seem, has returned to Scotland.
A happy ending, both for Macbeth and Duncan.
But we are merely in the second scene of the first act!

The purpose of Exposition, as I have said, is to introduce character, event; to define the conventions of the work.

Note that in approximately four minutes of stage time, Shakespeare has introduced three witches, Duncan, his son, several noblemen, a bleeding captain, and has *deliberately* held back from introducing the title role of the play, allowing only a captain and a king to characterize him, and the witches to seek him out for an as yet undisclosed purpose.

Through setting, Shakespeare has defined and contrasted the order of the court with the villainies of nature.

Moreover, *all the dramatic action has occurred off-stage* (the witches' spell; the battle itself). Yet Shakespeare's use of these expository scenes is so active, so dynamic, that we are thrust into the *immediacy of these events*, even though we still do not know what they are, where they are going, or what Macbeth is like.

Thus far, what narrative conventions have we, as an audience, accepted?

1. The potential topsy-turvy influence of malignant elements upon the drama;
2. A rapid movement of events, shifting from one setting to another.

Before we continue our analysis of the uses of exposition, I would like to call your attention to the use of *cutting between scenes*.

Cutting Between Scenes

For some reason, very few screenwriters seem to have taken advantage of one of the greatest strengths of dramatic structure (and of which Shakespeare himself has left us a great many stunning examples): the use of cutting between scenes.

The dramatic and visual note at the end of scene A *so clearly will effect how we as an audience enter Scene B*. The note, last line or image of scene A creates, by its link with the first note, first line or image of Scene B, an unspoken metaphor of the drama, or a very specific analogy, *which easily becomes the hidden or inner structure of the work*.

For example, examine the end of I,i and the beginning of I,ii in *Macbeth*.

The last lines of Scene 1 are the witches' chant "Fair is foul, and foul is fair, hover through the fog and filthy air." Almost immediately thereafter horns are sounded: the King appears with attendants. Then, from the opposite side of the stage, a bleeding captain appears.

KING
What bloody man is that?

What subtle link exists for our senses, between the witches' exit and the King's entrance?

Foul, fog, filth, the shrieking of the wind, a battle, the sound of horns, a procession, then the entrance of the bleeding Captain.

Even though the Captain has little to do with the three witches or their state, he might well enter from the same side of the stage from which they exited, *emerging,* in effect, *from their condition*. A subtle link thus is created between the witches' power and the Captain's state, *even if the narrative line does not draw attention to this*.

The cutting between scenes 1 and 2 implies a realm of bloody being, and creates a metaphor of the world of (super)natural action.

The analogy or metaphor, however, is never directly stated. It is implied.

Note that *the characters themselves* are not even aware of it. (How could they be aware, involved as they are in the events, which is precisely where any good dramatist wants them to be?)

Where and what you want an audience to see and to feel—your point-of-view towards the characters and event— are subtly hidden in that microsecond shift between scenes. Such cuts have a cumulative effect upon an audience, for they create the underpinnings, the substructure of the drama itself. The senses of the audience *intuit* the reaction you require.

In every film I write—knowing how potent a device the cut between scenes can be—I review the end of each scene, the beginning of the next, seeing if a thematic metaphor, or character analogy may serve as a link between sections, creating the subtext of the drama. (Such cutting became a structural necessity in the adaptation I'd written of Vonnegut's *Slaughterhouse Five*, examples of which will be considered in Part Three.)

But what about the cuts between scenes I,ii and I,iii in *Macbeth*?

Note the last couplet of I,ii, and see how the cut itself is used as a plot device:

ROSS
    I'll see it done.
KING
    What he hath lost noble Macbeth hath won.
                    [Exeunt.]

At the beginning of the next scene, the witches enter.

Before they even speak, we know they will be meeting "noble Macbeth." How nobly will he behave, once the witches have done with him? Will he have "won" the witches? Our expectations are high. And, to tease us further, Shakespeare immediately veers away from our expectations.

1st WITCH
    Where hast thou been, sister?
2nd WITCH
    Killing swine.

Shoptalk among the Nasties, which continues for thirty-two lines.

By deliberately *avoiding resolving our immediate expectations*, Shakespeare builds our expectations even higher, to the sound of a drum. The author could not have accomplished this piece of suspense had he ended on a line *which did not refer so specifically to Macbeth*. (Note the natural vocal pause as one reads the line aloud: "What he hath lost (pause) noble Macbeth hath won.")

What does nobility have to do with consorting with witches?

Shakespeare's strength lies not only in knowing when to leave a scene and how to get into the next, but also *in building the subtext conditions of the world he is depicting*—by a knowledge of how to create visual and vocal tensions in the cuts between scenes.

Notice also how this cutting has prepared us, in the case of Macbeth, to accept *the use of irony* as a commentary upon the action.

If noble Macbeth, according to the King, has won a title, what will he win when he meets the witches? Shakespeare prepares us to listen carefully to Duncan. The King's perceptions of Macbeth, however honest and fair and, on the face of Macbeth's action, correct, will be proved most incorrect.

Through his use of cutting, Shakespeare is leading us to accept two levels of reality operating at cross-purposes: the solid world of Duncan and the court, and the topsy-turvy world of the witches.

In Part Three, we will discuss the substructure of the screenplay at greater length. For the moment, realize that the proper use of cutting between scenes can help develop theme, imply hidden atmospheres, and point the audience specifically towards the narrative tone of the work.

But we have left the three weird sisters on the heath. A drum sounds. The witches prepare to meet Macbeth.

Resolution of Exposition

I,iii

3RD WITCH
A drum, a drum!
Macbeth doth come.

ALL
The weird sisters, hand in hand,
Posters of the sea and land,
Thus do go about, about,
Thrice to thine, and thrice to mine,
And thrice again, to make up nine.
Peace! The charm's wound up.
[*Enter* MACBETH *and* BANQUO.]

MACBETH
So foul and fair a day I have not seen.

BANQUO
How far is't called to Forres? What are these,
So withered and so wild in their attire
That look not like th' inhabitants o' th' earth
And yet are on't? Live you, or are you aught
That man may question? You seem to understand
    me,
By each at once her choppy finger laying
Upon her skinny lips. You should be women,

And yet your beards forbid me to interpret
That you are so.

MACBETH   Speak, if you can. What are you?

1ST WITCH
All hail, Macbeth! Hail to thee, Thane of Glamis!

2ND WITCH
All hail, Macbeth! Hail to thee, Thane of Cawdor!

3RD WITCH
All hail, Macbeth, that shalt be King hereafter!

BANQUO
Good sir, why do you start and seem to fear
Things that do sound so fair? I' th' name of truth,
Are ye fantastical, or that indeed
Which outwardly ye show? My noble partner
You greet with present grace and great prediction
Of noble having and of royal hope,
That he seems rapt withal. To me you speak not.
If you can look into the seeds of time
And say which grain will grow and which will
    not,
Speak then to me, who neither beg nor fear
Your favors nor your hate.

1ST WITCH   Hail!

2ND WITCH   Hail!

3RD WITCH   Hail!

1ST WITCH
Lesser than Macbeth, and greater.

2ND WITCH
Not so happy, yet much happier.

3RD WITCH
Thou shalt get kings, though thou be none.
So all hail, Macbeth and Banquo!

1ST WITCH
Banquo and Macbeth, all hail!

MACBETH
Stay, you imperfect speakers, tell me more:
By Sinel's death I know I am Thane of Glamis,
But how of Cawdor? The Thane of Cawdor lives,
A prosperous gentleman; and to be King
Stands not within the prospect of belief,
No more than to be Cawdor. Say from whence

You owe this strange intelligence, or why
Upon this blasted heath you stop our way
With such prophetic greeting. Speak, I charge
you.

[WITCHES *vanish*.]

The first words Macbeth speaks—"So foul and fair a day I have not seen"—*directly links him with the witches,* placing him in psychic sync with this supernatural condition.

And still Shakespeare continues to withhold Macbeth's physical identity from the audience until the witches hail him directly. Two men have appeared, and ten lines are spoken before their identities are revealed. Even then, Shakespeare's only stroke of characterization remains a subtle one ("So foul and fair a day"), which still reveals little about the man.

The witches hail Macbeth.

He "starts and seems to fear" their glamorous prophecies. Banquo himself, urging the witches to give him prophecy as well, calls Macbeth "noble." As the weird sisters start to vanish, Macbeth strains forward, demanding that they explain themselves. Unlike the florid rhetoric of Banquo's questioning, Macbeth's lines are forceful, direct, completely to the point. In his recovery he shows himself a man of action.

But too late. The witches have vanished.

The confrontation between Macbeth and the agents of darkness is a magnificent *example of resolution of exposition, and of preparation for further exposition*.

How has Shakespeare accomplished this?

In I,i he planted the possibility of confrontation between the witches and Macbeth.

In I,iii the confrontation occurred. More, he planted further exposition by hailing Macbeth as King.

And yet, Shakespeare has not directly defined Macbeth as anything more than a man of action.

In I,ii we had learned (without the witches even being present) that Macbeth has been named Thane of Cawdor. The witches' prophecy already has come true, even before they themselves had pronounced it. With this resolution, our focus subtly begins to shift from events which are forced upon Macbeth, to Macbeth's response itself. Soon he will move from passivity to action.

Exposition has an orchestral, harmonic effect upon the viewer, its rhythm occupying three stages: preparation, development, and resolution.

Thus far, from Scene I,i to line 79 of Scene I,iii:

Preparation 1:	Witches desire to meet with Macbeth; Macbeth is given the title of Thane of Cawdor.
Development:	The witches meet in I,iii, awaiting Macbeth.
Resolution:	Witches greet Macbeth as Thane of Cawdor.
Preparation 2:	Witches also greet Macbeth as King.

Note that Shakespeare *still* has told us little about the man, withholding his nature from our eyes *until all the pieces of the play are in place, and Macbeth may reveal himself*. Once "the charm's wound up," (i.e., all the characters are introduced, the action defined), *the play almost will seem to write itself*, the action seemingly inevitable.

I have stressed the first ten minutes of playing time as being the most crucial.

Without a doubt, the most difficult (and exciting) aspect of dramatic writing is the construction of the initial scenes.

Somehow they must appear effortless, unself-conscious, flowing as naturally as the winds. In other words, your use of exposition not only must advance the drama, but also (and at the same time) *define* it. A well-developed first act, with characters and actions in place, will make the writing of the second (and third or fourth) acts so much easier.

RULE: Any script with trouble at the end *inevitably has trouble at the beginning*!

In other words, the characters and events were *never* clearly defined, the exposition was *weak*, and therefore supported an easily collapsible structure.

It is axiomatic that trouble at the end means trouble at the beginning.

Further Examples of Character & Scene-Setting

Approximately 7-8 minutes of playing time have elapsed in *Macbeth*.

The witches have vanished.

I, iii (continued)
BANQUO
> The earth hath bubbles as the water has,
> And these are of them. Whither are they
> vanished?

MACBETH
> Into the air, and what seemed corporeal melted
> As breath into the wind. Would they had stayed!

BANQUO
> Were such things here as we do speak about?
> Or have we eaten on the insane root
> That takes the reason prisoner?

MACBETH
> Your children shall be kings.

BANQUO   You shall be King.

MACBETH
> And Thane of Cawdor too. Went it not so?

BANQUO
> To th' selfsame tune and words. Who's here?
> [*Enter* ROSS *and* ANGUS.]

After the confrontation with the witches, a high point has been reached. Therefore, Shakespeare gives us eight lines of *pausa*, where the event has time to sink into both the characters' minds, and ours. The repetition of the prophecies is meant to ensure that we in the audience know what the stakes are. (And where we might think Macbeth would reveal his nature, he *doesn't*!)

> **I, iii** (continued)
> **ROSS**
>> The King hath happily received, Macbeth,
>> The news of thy success; and when he reads
>> Thy personal venture in the rebels' fight,
>> His wonders and his praises do contend
>> Which should be thine or his. Silenced with that,
>> In viewing o'er the rest o' th' selfsame day,
>> He finds thee in the stout Norweyan ranks,
>> Nothing afeard of what thyself didst make,
>> Strange images of death. As thick as tale
>> Came post with post, and every one did bear
>> Thy praises in his kingdom's great defense
>> And poured them down before him.
>
> **ANGUS**   We are sent
>> To give thee from our royal master thanks;
>> Only to herald thee into his sight,
>> Not pay thee.
>
> **ROSS**
>> And for an earnest of a greater honor,
>> He bade me, from him, call thee Thane of Cawdor;
>> In which addition, hail, most worthy Thane,
>> For it is thine.
>
> **BANQUO**   What, can the devil speak true?

Ross's long speech gives us a chance to stare at Macbeth, to watch his gestures, to see exactly what kind of man he is. Obviously he does not react, for Angus jumps Ross's lines, cutting short the man's rhetorical posture. Ross, not to be outdone, "tops" Ross, and presents Macbeth with his title. Note the repetition of the word "Thane;" how, the first time it is spoken, it seems almost a throwaway line. Then, by setting off "hail" between commas, Shakespeare slows down the rush of speech, emphasizing the title *three times: "hail," "Thane," "thine."*

Banquo reacts unself-consciously, and perhaps ambiguously: "What, can the devil speak true?" Does he refer to the witches' prophecy or to the man himself?

Note how much more controlled Macbeth replies:

MACBETH
The Thane of Cawdor lives. Why do you dress me
In borrowed robes?
ANGUS   Who was the Thane lives yet,
But under heavy judgment bears that life
Which he deserves to lose. Whether he was
    combined
With those of Norway, or did line the rebel
With hidden help and vantage, or that with both
He labored in his country's wrack, I know not;
But treasons capital, confessed and proved,
Have overthrown him.
MACBETH [*Aside*]   Glamis, and Thane
of Cawdor—
The greatest is behind!
        [*To* ROSS *and* ANGUS] Thanks for your
        pains.
        [*Aside to* BANQUO]
Do you not hope your children shall be kings,
When those that gave the Thane of Cawdor to
    me
Promised no less to them?
BANQUO [*To* MACBETH]   That, trusted home,
Might yet enkindle you unto the crown,
Besides the Thane of Cawdor. But 'tis strange:
And oftentimes, to win us to our harm,
The instruments of darkness tell us truths,
Win us with honest trifles, to betray's
In deepest consequence.
Cousins, a word, I pray you.

The inner tumult has begun.
Is the greatest, indeed, behind?
Banquo seems to sense Macbeth's stirrings, and warns
him about the habits of the "instruments of darkness."
But Macbeth cannot be stopped:

MACBETH [*Aside*] Two truths are told,
As happy prologues to the swelling act
Of imperial theme.—I thank you, gentleman.—
[*Aside*] This supernatural soliciting
Cannot be ill, cannot be good. If ill,
Why hath it given me earnest of success,
Commencing in a truth? I am Thane of Cawdor.
If good, why do I yield to that suggestion
Whose horrid image doth unfix my hair
And make my seated heart knock at my ribs
Against the use of nature? Present fears
Are less than horrible imaginings.
My thought, whose murder yet is but fantastical,
Shakes so my single state of man that function
Is smothered in surmise and nothing is
But what is not.
BANQUO Look how our partner's rapt.

As if to ensure that the audience both feels and understands Macbeth's "horrible imaginings," Shakespeare frames Macbeth's aside by having Banquo point them out. Now all our attention is focused upon the man:

MACBETH [*Aside*]
If chance will have me King, why chance may
Crown me without my stir.
BANQUO New honors come upon him,
Like our strange garments, cleave not to their
Mould but with the aid of use.
MACBETH [*Aside*] Come what, come may,
Time and the hour runs through the roughest
day.
BANQUO
Worthy Macbeth, we stay upon your leisure.
MACBETH
Give me your favor. My dull brain was wrought
With things forgotten. King gentlemen, your pains
Are regist'red where every day I turn
The leaf to read them. Let us toward the King.
[*Aside to* BANQUO]

> Think upon what hath chanced, and at more
>   time,
> The interim having weighed it, let us speak
> Our free hearts each to other.
> **BANQUO**   Very gladly.
> **MACBETH**
> Till then, enough. — Come, friends. [*Exeunt.*]

By now I hope you have begun to read from within the text itself, noting how *events and characters* are *prepared, tension created* and *sustained*, and *exposition* of character and events *resolved*.

Also most likely you have begun to see how the cumulative effect of this threefold use of exposition (preparation; development; resolution) carries with it a dramatic pulse *that gives the scenes momentum and pace*. Shakespeare's brilliant use of exposition has an immediacy, a present tense-ness that sweeps the audience along with the action.

More Thoughts on the Scene

With the entrance of the noblemen Ross and Angus, this second beat of I,iii both wondrously and economically brings the world of the court directly into the domain of the witches, merging both worlds until each acts upon and affects the other—and all of this having been prepared for, both subtly and confidently, in the first two scenes. Certainly Shakespeare could have left the honors heaped upon Macbeth for the fourth scene, and delivered by Duncan himself. But by deliberately *forcing the event at the heath*—and shortly after the witches' exit—the author dramatizes the influence of the malign upon the future of Scotland. And since we already have learned in I,ii that Macbeth might be called Cawdor, the revelation in I,iii becomes less important than *Macbeth's own response to it*.

Shakespeare is preparing us to concentrate upon the physical and psychic actions of the brave, noble, valiant cousin, and worthy gentleman.

Macbeth is both watchful and clever in his response to the news that he has been made Thane of Cawdor.

Banquo is stunned, and inadvertently blurts "What, can the devil speak true?" Next, Banquo, in an aside, tells Macbeth that the "instruments of darkness" might prove false. Macbeth himself realizes that fair may well be foul, that nothing is what it seems. He becomes frightened by the unsettledness which has begun to penetrate his thoughts—implying the murder of Duncan. His confusion is understandable, his response to the others courtly, his warmth towards Banquo moving. And yet in the course of this, Shakespeare has planted a character point that is critical to the event:

MACBETH
> If chance will have me King, why chance may
> Crown me *without my stir*.

Otherwise . . .

Buried in this scene is the *first active step* of Macbeth's which leads to a bloody throne.

At this point Macbeth has revealed himself to be an ambitious, thoughtful, clever, and frightened man, whose truest story is about to begin.

But the basic exposition of the play is not yet complete: we still do not know what Macbeth plans to do (if anything at all). The prophecies spoken, tokens reaped, the scene now shifts from the "blasted heath" to the comforts of the court.

I,iv
[*Flourish. Enter* KING DUNCAN, LENNOX,
    MALCOLM, DONALBAIN, *and attendants.*]

KING
>   Is execution done on Cawdor? Are not
>   Those in commission yet returned?

MALCOLM   My liege,
>   They are not yet come back. But I have spoke
>   With one that saw him die; who did report
>   That very frankly he confessed his treasons,
>   Implored your Highness' pardon, and set forth
>   A deep repentance. Nothing in his life
>   Became him like the leaving it. He died
>   As one that had been studied in his death
>   To throw away the dearest thing he owed
>   As 'twere a careless trifle.

KING   There's no art
>   To find the mind's construction in the face.
>   He was a gentleman on whom I built
>   An absolute trust.

>   [*Enter* MACBETH, BANQUO, ROSS, *and*
>   ANGUS.]

>   O worthiest cousin . . .

As *cutting between scenes* plays an effective role in storytelling, so too does *cutting within the same scene* aid us in character delineation.

Macbeth's entrance on the phrase "absolute trust" is not to be overlooked. *HOW A CHARACTER ENTERS, AND ON WHAT LINE, AND ON WHAT ACTION, CAN EITHER DIRECTLY STATE OR IMPLY TO AN AUDIENCE EXACTLY WHAT YOU WISH THEM TO KNOW.*

After Macbeth's confusion on the heath, his "horrible imaginings," this is a bold character touch indeed. What kind of man is Duncan? Is he so artful in his understanding of human nature that he builds his trust upon a traitor? And now salutes a traitor-to-be?

KING
>   . . . The sin of my ingratitude even now
>   Was heavy on me. Thou art so far before
>   That swiftest wing of recompense is slow
>   To overtake thee. Would thou hadst less deserved,
>   That the proportion both of thanks and payment

> Might have been mine! Only I have left to say,
> More is thy due than more than all can pay.

MACBETH
> The service and the loyalty I owe,
> In doing it pays itself. Your Highness' part
> Is to receive our duties, and our duties
> Are to your throne and state children and servants,
> Which do but what they should by doing every
>   thing
> Safe toward your love and honor.

KING   Welcome hither.
> I have begun to plant thee and will labor
> To make thee full of growing. Noble Banquo,
> That hast no less deserved nor must be known
> No less to have done so, let me enfold thee
> And hold thee to my heart.

BANQUO   There if I grow,
> The harvest is your own.

KING   My plenteous joys,
> Wanton in fullness, seek to hide themselves
> In drops of sorrow. Sons, kinsmen, thanes,
> And you whose places are the nearest, know
> We will establish our estate upon
> Our eldest, Malcolm, whom we name hereafter
> The Prince of Cumberland; which honor must
> Not unaccompanied invest him only,
> But signs of nobleness, like stars, shall shine
> On all deservers. From hence to Inverness,
> And bind us further to you.

MACBETH
> The rest is labor which is not used for you.
> I'll be myself the harbinger, and make joyful
> The hearing of my wife with your approach;
> So, humbly take my leave.

Macbeth states that he has merely done his duty to
the King and his children. *Almost immediately* the King
deals a body-blow to Macbeth: Malcolm, Duncan's eldest
son, will be named Prince of Cumberland, and thereafter
King of Scotland. Almost immediately Macbeth rushes off,
scarcely able to contain his rage. No longer will he wait for

chance to crown him, for ambition has become his chief obsession.

This second character revelation (the broiling ambition of Macbeth) is about to be further planted. After Macbeth's exit, to treachery's true domain, the King states: "He is so valiant . . . it is a banquet to me." Again, note Shakespeare's intentional use of irony.

The action, at this point, is in full acceleration:

KING   My worthy Cawdor!
MACBETH [*Aside*]
    The Prince of Cumberland—that is a step
    On which I must fall down or else o'erleap,
    For in my way it lies. Stars, hide your fires;
    Let not light see my black and deep desires.
    The eye wink at the hand; yet let that be
    Which the eye fears, when it is done, to see.
                                            [*Exit.*]
KING
    True, worthy Banquo: he is full so valiant,
    And in his commendations I am fed;
    It is a banquet to me. Let's after him,
    Whose care is gone before to bid us welcome.
    It is a peerless kinsman.   [*Flourish. Exeunt.*]

Now, perhaps in the most graceful expository stroke of the play, Shakespeare reveals to us Macbeth's inner state of mind during his meeting with the witches but without Macbeth himself being present to reveal it!

At the same time Shakespeare introduces us to one of the greatest witches of all drama, Macbeth's lovely Lady.

I,v
[*Enter* MACBETH's WIFE, *alone, with a letter.*]
LADY MACBETH [*Reads*] "They met me in the
    day of success; and I have learned by the perfect'st
    report they have more in them than mortal
    knowledge. When I burned in desire to question
    them further, they made themselves air, into
    which they vanished. Whiles I stood rapt in the

wonder of it, came missives from the King, who
all-hailed me Thane of Cawdor, by which title,
before, these weird sisters saluted me, and re-
ferred me to the coming on of time with 'Hail,
King that shalt be!' This have I thought good to
deliver thee, my dearest partner of greatness,
that thou mightst not lose the dues of rejoicing
by being ignorant of what greatness is promised
thee. Lay it to thy heart, and farewell."
Glamis thou art, and Cawdor, and shalt be
What thou art promised. Yet do I fear thy nature.
It is too full o' th' milk of human kindness
To catch the nearest way. Thou wouldst be great,
Art not without ambition, but without
The illness should attend it. What thou wouldst
    highly,
That wouldst thou holily; wouldst not play false,
And yet wouldst wrongly win. Thou'ldst have,
    great Glamis,
That which cries "Thus thou must do if thou have
    it;
And that which rather thou dost fear to do
Than wishest should be undone." Hie thee hither,
That I may pour my spirits in thine ear
And chastise with the valor of my tongue
All that impedes thee from the golden round
Which fate and metaphysical aid doth seem
To have thee crowned withal.
    [*Enter* MESSENGER.] What is your tidings?

Imagine: the fourth scene was filled with the pomp
and trappings of male authority.

The fifth begins with *a woman alone*, reading a letter.

How splendidly Shakespeare has orchestrated his drama,
for this scene is the last remaining piece of major exposition to be played before the action is swept along by
Macbeth's desires.

To begin the scene with a solitary woman, in contrast
to the masculine world we have seen, is stagecraft of the
highest sort—especially since the woman proves to be
more than interesting.

We hear her husband's letter.

It is a direct report, almost a playing-down of the broiling desire and confusion he had felt after hearing the prophecies. The near-childlike simplicity of the writing is in wonderful contrast to Lady Macbeth's response.

We have watched King, Captain, witches greet Macbeth for his present actions and future conquest. Now Shakespeare rips through the courtiers' trappings and gives us the most honest and penetrating view of Macbeth as a man, known to a woman. For only the woman would understand that his nature's "too full o' th' milk of human kindness," that his ambition lacks "the illness" to give it force. Oh, how she wishes her husband would arrive quickly, that she could encourage his ambition, could strengthen him to fulfill the greatest prophecy of all: to become King, (but through an act of murder)!

Suddenly her thoughts are interrupted. (Again, *note the rhythm of these entrances and exits*, how they serve to develop tension while advancing plot.)

I,v

MESSENGER

The King comes here to-night.

LADY MACBETH

Thou'rt mad to say it!
Is not thy master with him? who, were't so,
Would have informed for preparation.

MESSENGER

So please you, it is true. Our Thane is coming.
One of my fellows had the speed of him,
Who, almost dead for breath, had scarcely more
Than would make up his message.

LADY MACBETH

Give him tending;
He brings great news.

[*Exit* MESSENGER.]

The Messenger's line is almost a completion of Lady Macbeth's thought. Her "Thou'rt mad to say it!" is a brave leap into the darkest fears of her mind, the knowledge of which *startles her* into domesticity.

If the Messenger is correct, why hasn't Macbeth himself informed her of Duncan's coming? (This domestic touch—Hubby is bringing home the Boss for dinner, and forgets to tell the little woman—is black comedy itself.)

Once again the woman stands alone, but no longer is she the sweet, domesticated Lady we had seen 35 lines ago, waiting like Penelope for her hero to return from the wars.

I,v
LADY MACBETH
> The raven himself is hoarse
> That croaks the fatal entrance of Duncan
> Under my battlements. Come, you spirits
> That tend on mortal thoughts, unsex me here,
> And fill me from the crown to the toe top-full
> Of direst cruelty. Make thick my blood;
> Stop up th' access and passage to remorse,
> That no compunctious visitings of nature
> Shake my fell purpose nor keep peace between
> The effect and it. Come to my woman's breasts
> And take my milk for gall, you murd'ring ministers,
> Wherever in your sightless substances
> You wait on nature's mischief. Come, thick night,
> And pall thee in the dunnest smoke of hell,
> That my keen knife see not the wound it makes,
> Nor heaven peep through the blanket of the dark
> To cry "Hold, hold!"
> [*Enter* MACBETH.] Great Glamis! worthy Cawdor!

We have heard the witches' invocation before, and it is mild by comparison with Lady Macbeth's. More, it defines the witches as *passive* agents of a darkly magical operation. Lady Macbeth, however, *actively* invokes the spirits to fill her with smoking hell, to change the nature of her sex (Meek, is it? And docile?), to poison her breasts, to become the essence of murder itself. At the height of this extraordinary demonic takeover, Macbeth appears, and his "born-again" wife rhapsodizes:

> Great Glamis! worthy Cawdor!
> Greater than both, by the all-hail hereafter.

Note how Macbeth's shock is implied in his wife's following lines, his fear and concern for her rapture:

LADY MACBETH
> Thy letters have transported me beyond
> This ignorant present, and I feel now
> The future in an instant.

Fair indeed has become foul (and all the more reason for Lady Macbeth to be played by a strikingly beautiful actress—admiration for Judith Anderson aside), and the future is in the present.

MACBETH   My dearest love,
> Duncan comes here tonight.
LADY MACBETH
> And when goes hence?
MACBETH   Tomorrow, as he purposes.
LADY MACBETH
> O, never
> Shall sun that morrow see!

In 3½ lines (count your iambs), *Shakespeare now reveals the intention of the plot by exposing the deepest cravings of the principals' hearts.*

This could not have been accomplished had he not prepared us through the expository means examined in the previous pages.

Everything now is in place for the final prophecy to be fulfilled.

Or nearly everything.

Shakespeare yet has one more touch to make and which, ironically, will recall Duncan's own words about the first traitorous Thane of Cawdor:

LADY MACBETH
> Your face, my Thane, is as a book where men

> May read strange matters. To beguile the time,
> Look like the time; bear welcome in your eye,
> Your hand, your tongue; look like th' innocent
> flower,
> But be the serpent under't. He that's coming
> Must be provided for; and you shall put
> This night's great business into my dispatch,
> Which shall to all our nights and days to come
> Give solely sovereign sway and masterdom.

MACBETH
> We will speak further.

LADY MACBETH
> Only look up clear!
> To alter favor ever is to fear.
> Leave all the rest to me.

> [*Exeunt.*]

This clearly is Lady Macbeth's scene.

She has entered the stage innocently reading a letter, seemingly dwarfed by the castle walls, a woman all too soft for the bloody business of battles. Yet she leaves the stage with her own innocence murdered by her own hands.

The Messenger's entrance was a device used *not only to accelerate the plot, but also to give the Lady (and the audience) time to digest the letter, and then to raise her will for demonic invocation*.

Macbeth's entrance at the height of her cry is almost operatically orchestrated, her love now overwhelmingly erotic, their complicity near complete.

All is in readiness.

Through the brilliantly orchestrated use of exposition, Shakespeare has introduced his characters, themes, events.

He has stated the conventions of the drama.

He has created a fair-is-foul atmosphere, and a horribly ironic tone for the piece. And, if my line count is correct, the four scenes play *in slightly less than twenty minutes*. The "crucial ten minutes" theory *still* stands, for it takes us midway through the third scene, the all-hail prophecies, where everyone but Lady Macbeth has been introduced, the action prepared, and conventions set. (In film, of course, the visual images themselves may shorten much of the dialogue.)

Our excitement at the mounting action is due to the careful, teasing revelation of Macbeth's character, and his wife's zealous, incautious love.

We have become aware that Macbeth's character is, in fact, the event. (When we study *characterization*, we will return to Lady Macbeth again.)

Now that you've an idea of the crucial opening ten minutes; the strengths of cutting between scenes; the dramatic uses of entrances and exits; now that you have examined the why-and-how of exposition (used, in *Macbeth*, to great dramatic effect), you owe yourselves a treat.

Go to a movie.

Enjoy it in the light of this process of analysis.

Ask yourself:

How does the author introduce character?

What is the character's relationship to setting?

How does the setting influence character?

What kind of expository devices does the author use to develop story and character(s)?

Through analysis of these opening gambits, you will begin to understand if you are dealing with an artist, an artisan, a hack or a simple fool. And no matter how clever the initial moves, the rest must follow faithfully in characterization, theme, and tone.

This matter of consistency is so simple that often it is forgotten!

(Recently I saw a play in New York that was billed as a bittersweet comedy. The first act, indeed, was both bittersweet and comic. The second act suddenly became "profound and meaningful." Needless to say, by switching conventions halfway through the play, the author lost the audience—who had been conditioned in the first act to accept her tone, and did so, willingly.)

As you begin to analyze the "crucial ten minutes," as

well as the opening gambits, note if the tone of the environment and characterizations are *consistent* throughout the piece. If not consistent, *why not*? If so, *how*?

To recapitulate:

A. Exposition serves to introduce the audience to:
   1. Characters,
   2. Events,
   3. Themes,
   4. Physical and metaphysical conventions of the work.

B. Exposition accomplishes this through the devices of:
   1. Atmosphere, or mood,
   2. Dramatic use of setting,
   3. *Gradual* manipulation of event,
   4. *Gradual* manipulation of character,
   5. Cutting between scenes,
   6. The use of entrances and exits within scenes,
   7. Language.

C. Exposition creates a *rhythm or pace* through the use of:
   1. Preparation (of event, character),
   2. Development (of event, character),
   3. Resolution (of event, character).

A parting poem before you go to the movies:
    If Exposition dumbly struts before thee,
    The author's work is sure to lull and bore thee;
    If Exposition's hidden from thine eyes,
    The author is indeed a Mage, and wise;
    If Revelation rolls as it is meant,
    Then Character itself's the bold Event;
    If Revelation seems a silly trick,
    Then—O Contempt!—it's just another flic.

Characterization

"Birth, copulation and death—
That's all the facts, when you get to brass tacks."

True, we are born, mature, procreate, die, but in that process there are a thousand births, copulations, and deaths in our hopes; a million births, copulations, and deaths in our minds, with a trillion variables directed towards us during this process. (If life indeed were as reductive as T.S. Eliot has written, then it is curious why he himself ever bothered to write a line of poetry, or to introduce the works of others.)

As long as people wake up in the morning, grumble or grin, walk the sunny side of the street, decide to covet their neighbor's wives, kill their husbands or become saints, the writer never is at a loss for wonder—much less, for material.

Yet Eliot himself pointed to a dramatic arc, a revelation of character and event in his line, "Birth, copulation and death." There's a tale in four words, and it implies a *movement of character* from start to finish. Simplistic as this may seem, the art of characterization is both nothing and a great deal more.

The art consists of walking a character across the street and, in the process, altering his perceptions. By the time he lifts a foot onto the curb, he will never be the same. Either events will have forced him to live in the world differently, or he himself will have rearranged events with willful momentum.

Nobody leaves the world in the manner in which he entered it.

And few characters in fiction are any different.

If you think of most films—however bad—*something happens*. And that *something* happens to the principal characters.

Let's discuss some great films:

In Bergman's *Wild Strawberries*, Professor Borg is depicted as the *summa* of all male qualities: striving, ambitious, rational, clear-headed. And, because of this, a victim of loneliness. By the end of the movie, he has learned to accommodate tenderness, mercy, forgiveness, kindness. And is no longer lonely. The "wild strawberries," his own "female" nature, are finally tended.

In Fellini's and Flaiano's *8½*, Guido is unable to make sense of the elements of his life and fantasies. He is, therefore, unable to create. At the film's resolution, he has learned to accept his own confusions, and to embrace the paradoxical aspects of his life. A new and rich film, therefore, has begun.

In Richard Rush and Lawrence Marcus's *The Stunt Man*, Cameron views the world as a paranoid rush about to mow him down. By the end of the film, he is made to realize that his paranoia was a *choice*, not a universal condition—and he survives his own near-death.

In Woody Allen and Marshall Brickman's *Manhattan*, our hero learns that true love is not ambitious or grasping.

In *High Noon*, the ex-sheriff refuses to fight; is forced to fight; spurns the fight; grapples with his own fears; and, in the final fight, emerges victorious.

Characterization consists of taking a principal from one point of reference and gracefully flinging him to another. From *Oedipus Rex* to *One Flew Over The Cuckoo's Nest*, the art of characterization requires the gradual stripping away of preconceptions, wearing down the armor until a newer, truer reality is seen. It may not be the ultimate reality, but the character has certainly been brought closer to it. Whether the writing is comic, melodramatic or tragic, few characters leave the frame as they first entered.*

---

*I will now contradict myself.
Waiting for Godot and *Billy Budd*, for example, are fixed in time, and derive their tension from the tragicomic maintenance

In the section on exposition, I stated that Shakespeare's skill in characterization was due to his ability *to make character indistinguishable from event;* that this type of dramaturgy gave to his work a sense of immediacy, of present tense. The drama, moreover, seemed to depend upon the revelation of a trait (or traits) of character which, upon contact with a specific event, set the theatrical chemistry in motion. Thus character became indistinguishable from event.

No matter from whose point-of-view the drama is written:

Character *is* Event.
Event *is* Change.
Character *is* Change.

How to write characters?

As obvious as this may seem, you must first know who the characters are, their origins and hopes; then you must know how the characters are going to end.

Between these points lies the drama, the *process* of characterization.

Earlier I said that I rarely began to write until I had heard the voice of my protagonist.

That voice told me who he or she was, and gave me a clue to his or her origins.

That voice gave me a peek into heart and psyche.

By this I do not mean that I sat in a corner and did nothing until, like Joan of Arc, the "voices" began to sound. Rather, I wrote character sketches, snatches of

---

of status quo. But eventually a leaf does appear, even though Godot doesn't; eventually Captain Vere will die and be called to account for his conscience; in other words, even though characterization in *Godot* consists in waiting, and in *Budd* consists in singlemindedly grasping the moral order of the present as both fixed and eternal, there *is* eventual, off-stage, off-page change. Even in *The Cherry Orchard*, where much of the rolling, active drama occurs off-stage, eventually it does burst into the garden to threaten the stability of the human estate.

dialogue. I imagined the character making love, walking the streets, buying a hat, *anything* that would tell me *something* about his or her perceptions.

In my first novel, *She Let Him Continue* (filmed as *Pretty Poison*), I knew that a boy would meet a girl, that the boy would fall in love with the girl, and that both boy and girl would kill the girl's mother. I also knew that it would be the girl's idea.

I based this story on a real occurrence in New England. But I heard no "voice" (and therefore knew no character) until I read that the young man in the real incident had told a reporter he himself was a C.I.A. agent.

At that point, the writing began. The *folie à deux* emerged from *his* fantasies, and from *her* own very real boredom.

In the film *Mister Ambassador*, I knew that my hero, Wesley Prewitt, Jr., was a bright, good-natured, curious and useless young man. When he became a politically appointed ambassador to an equally good-natured and useless island in the South Pacific, I knew that his curiosity eventually would change the face of the island. His good nature and desire to be useful, therefore, would trip him up.

In the instances of both novel and film my principal concern was to make sure that action sprang directly from character. I did this first by defining the character, then by deciding how I wanted him to finish. Once I heard his "voice," I knew that I could accomplish the in-between; that the work would possess an immediacy, would actively involve the audience as the tale unfolded.

And the greater the change in character, the greater the peaks of the events.

And the greater the degree of audience participation.

Another point: In *She Let Him Continue* I found Dennis Pitts's fantasies bizarre and amusing. I was also a bit in love with his girlfriend, Sue Ann Stepanek. (Amoral, perhaps; but if *I* couldn't love her, then *Dennis* certainly wouldn't.) In *Mister Ambassador* I did not find it difficult to relate to Wesley's two left feet, and his goodwill. The more he screwed up, the more I liked him. His motives were as pure as his actions were cockeyed. *Being emotionally involved with my characters, I stood a better chance of involving the audience as well.*

Taking Your First Steps in Characterization

1. Through sketches, jottings, dreams, learn the voices and, therefore, the identities of your principal characters.
2. Know *where* and *how* the characters end.
3. As you move them to that end, *enjoy them*.

In the wings lurks another rule:

Do not let the characters know what is going to happen to them until the final page, curtain, or fade out.

Since they will genuinely remain in the dark, so will the audience.

I am implying here a certain life-choice.

Perhaps it craves definition: if I knew where I would be six months or a year from now, I think I'd pack it in. For me the pleasure of living lies in its very uncertainty. I'm not nostalgic for the "good old days," since I can't recall when those "old days" were any better or worse than these new days. They were and are, simply, days, and each day presents an exceptional novelty or horror, joy or enthusiasm. Each day varies.

If you disagree and consider me fantastic, try this exercise:

Write a character who believes in the *status quo*, and who is living his life accordingly.

Then give him a heart attack.

Or have his son develop a curious lust for ex-President Nixon. The basis of comedy and tragedy, *in either situation, played either way*, lies therein.

* * *

I like Lady Macbeth.

For over four hundred years she's had a terrible press.

I believe Shakespeare found her amusing, if not poignant, as well.

Most directors and performers, however, consider her the Bitch Witch of All Times. Her character is rendered grizzly, dripping in blood; her language seemingly steeped in gore (when it's more often steeped in bad line directions); her very gestures a tribute to man's worst hell-imaginings.

Why is this so?

Because few directors, performers or, for that matter, readers have considered Shakespeare's *characterization* in and of itself. Shakespeare's method should move us, in our regard for the Lady, from awe and horror to intense pity.

Lady Macbeth appears *only eight times* in the play.

It is one of the shortest protagonist roles in dramatic literature—a brilliant feat of characterization.

In those eight scenes, Lady Macbeth moves through five distinct emotional and physical states, to her death.

Shakespeare leads her before our eyes from a loving wife possessed by her husband's ambitions; to a courteous Queen; to a wife concerned for her own husband's sanity; to a pitiful figure tormented by her own howling guilts; to a dying woman.

The movement is as linear and clear as it is passionate.

Lady Macbeth is an example of astonishing characterization, of masterly writing control. How could we pity a woman who has invoked demons, and who has remarked, after Duncan's murder, "I never thought the old man to have so much blood in him?"

And yet we do.

If Shakespeare's dramatic intention is followed and, literally, acted upon, she will deserve all our pity.

By studying Shakespeare's characterization of Lady Macbeth, we will see how the dramatist shifts our attention from horrible fascination to pity and awe, playing the woman from a variety of characters' points-of-view: not only her own, but also her husband's; a king's; several ladies'-in-waiting, and a doctor's.

(An interesting note: if, as an author, you are enthusiastic about your character, other fictional characters in the drama also will share your enthusiasm, helping you to give color and shading to the protagonist. As the character affects your creative life, so too will he or she affect the fictional lives of those who compose his or her world, *further ensuring the interaction of character and event*.)

Let us examine how Shakespeare moves his Lady from innocence to death, and then attempt to draw some general conclusions about the art of characterization.

King Duncan has arrived at Macbeth's castle:

I,vi: *(A GRACIOUS HOSTESS)*

KING   See, see, our honoured hostess!
The love that follows us sometime is our trouble,
Which still we thank as love. Herein I teach you
How you shall bid God 'ield us for your pains
And thank us for your trouble.
LADY MACBETH
All our service
In every point twice done, and then done double,
Were poor and single business to contend
Against those honors deep and broad wherewith
Your Majesty loads our house. For those of old,
And the late dignities heaped up to them,
We rest your hermits.
KING   Where's the Thane of Cawdor?
We coursed him at the heels and had a purpose
To be his purveyor; but he rides well,
And his great love, sharp as his spur, hath holp
   him
To his home before us. Fair and noble hostess,
We are your guest to-night.
LADY MACBETH
Your servants ever
Have theirs, themselves, and what is theirs, in
   compt,
To make their audit at your Highness' pleasure,
Still to return your own.
KING   Give me your hand.

> Conduct me to mine host; we love him highly
> And shall continue our graces towards him.
> By your leave, hostess.

> [*Exeunt.*]

Duncan's speech, grandiloquent and stately as it appears, is filled with unintentional irony. His opening address to Lady Macbeth,

> See, see, our honoured hostess!
> The love that follows us sometime is our trouble,
> Which still we thank as love

could easily refer to the Lady's love for her husband, which indeed will become *more than her trouble*: will become Duncan's, then her own death.

Lady Macbeth's response is controlled and elegant, a wife performing her duties both to King and Country. "Give me your hand," Duncan says. "Conduct me to mine host."

Which the Lady does, leading him, in terrible fact, to his murder.

That the scene not be rendered static, Shakespeare's bold use of irony *renders the woman's previous urgings to her husband persistent in our memory*, and gives the scene both tension and propulsion—which only will be relieved by Duncan's assassination.

Note that the last lines of Lady Macbeth in I,v, "Leave all the rest to me," is an *active* and *dynamic* response. Shakespeare then plays her character in this next scene as simple, obedient, dutiful. By this revelation of two faces, Shakespeare makes us aware of the extent of the Lady's cunning.

As we enter I,vii, the outward image of domesticity is renewed. Servants enter with torches, then dinner. A meal is in progress. Macbeth appears. He is confused, and rationalizes the possibilities of the murder.

I,vii: (*A CUNNING SERPENT*)
MACBETH   How now? What news?

LADY MACBETH
He has almost supped. Why have you left the
chamber?

MACBETH
Hath he asked for me?

LADY MACBETH
Know you not he has?

MACBETH
We will proceed no further in this business.
He hath honored me of late, and I have bought
Golden opinions from all sorts of people,
Which would be worn now in their newest gloss,
Not cast aside so soon.

Immediately Lady Macbeth is stunned by her husband's
change of plans:

LADY MACBETH
Was the hope drunk
Wherein you dressed yourself? Hath it slept
since?
And wakes it now to look so green and pale
At what it did so freely? From this time
Such I account thy love. Art thou afeard
To be the same in thine own act and valor
As thou art in desire? Wouldst thou have that
Which thou esteem'st the ornament of life,
And live a coward in thine own esteem,
Letting 'I dare not' wait upon 'I would,'
Like the poor cat i' th' adage?

MACBETH   Prithee peace!
I dare do all that may become a man;
Who dares do more is none.

LADY MACBETH
What beast was't then
That made you break this enterprise to me?
When you durst do it, then you were a man;
And to be more than what you were, you would
Be so much more the man. Nor time nor place
Did then adhere, and yet you would make both.

> They have made themselves, and that their fit-
> ness now
> Does unmake you. I have given suck, and know
> How tender 'tis to love the babe that milks me:
> I would, while it was smiling in my face,
> Have plucked my nipple from his boneless gums
> And dashed the brains out, had I so sworn as you
> Have done to this.

Lady Macbeth's fire, her cold rage, her knowledge and exploitation of her husband's weaknesses reveals a newer, all-consuming aspect of her character. Easily this can be traced to her invocation ("Come, you spirits...unsex me here"). Obviously the demonic prayer has worked. Unsexed, she would pluck her nipple from the gums of a feeding babe and dash his brains out if she'd sworn to perform the act of regicide:

MACBETH If we should fail?
LADY MACBETH We fail?
> But screw your courage to the sticking place
> And we'll not fail. When Duncan is asleep
> (Where to the rather shall his day's hard journey
> Soundly invite him), his two chamberlains
> Will I with wine and wassail so convince
> That memory, the warder of the brain,
> Shall be a fume, and the receipt of reason
> A limbeck only. When in swinish sleep
> Their drenched natures lies as in a death,
> What cannot you and I perform upon
> Th' unguarded Duncan? what not put upon
> His spongy officers, who shall bear the guilt
> Of our great quell?
MACBETH Bring forth men-children
> only;
> For thy undaunted mettle should compose
> Nothing but males.

Macbeth, however, who has not witnessed the takeover and so misreads his wife's cries for vitality, still seeing her as wife and mother, exclaims in admiration: "Bring forth men-children only"—stern and savage little males would he require, as ferociously uncompromising as she.

Clearly, Lady Macbeth is possessed, and her husband blinded by the illness of his own ambition.

Macbeth is a slow starter, and in his opening monologue shows by his own hesitancy that he yet may be a man of some moral substance.

Our sympathy remains *with his dilemma* until his wife calls his manhood into question, and moves him from inaction to potential violence.

> **MACBETH** Will it not be received,
>   When we have marked with blood those sleepy two
>   Of his own chamber and used their very daggers,
>   That they have done't?
> **LADY MACBETH**
>   Who dares receive it other,
>   As we shall make our griefs and clamor roar
>   Upon his death?
> **MACBETH** I am settled, and bend up
>   Each corporal agent to this terrible feat.
>   Away, and mock the time with fairest show;
>   False face must hide what the false heart doth know.
>   [*Exeunt.*]

In the exchange between Macbeth and his wife, *character both serves the event and is served by it*.

On the surface, what produces the exchange is Macbeth's sudden lack of courage, and his wife's violent response. This abrasiveness is *conflict*, the very substance of drama.

Interests clash.

Character is tested by the strength of events.

Note how the conflict see-saws between the characters; how the exchange of dialogue serves to move Macbeth from inaction to resolution; more, how it reveals the extent of Lady Macbeth's takeover.

This is a *miniature arc of conflict within the larger arc of the play*, whose very roots are nourished by characterization. In this *construction*, the conflict between Macbeth and spouse consists of a series of *rhythmic beats*, or gathering emotional heat. These *beats* are the direct result of the emotional and dramatic exchanges within the scene.

Let us re-examine the orchestration of this conflict:

1. Macbeth asks for news of the King. Lady Macbeth is annoyed that her husband has left his side.

2. Macbeth counters by refusing adamantly to go "further in this business." (Note how he will not even use the word "murder.")

3. Lady Macbeth is shocked by his new decision, and calls him cowardly and fearful. She challenges his very manhood.

4. Macbeth replies by saying it is his very manhood which keeps him from murder.

5. Lady Macbeth states that even *she* is more of a man than he, for had she sworn to do the deed, she would have kept her word. The violence of her response, the contrast between the frail woman and potent savage is so shocking that Macbeth no longer reacts emotionally against the murder but, rather, begins to work his way rationally and grimly towards regicide: what if they fail?

6. Lady Macbeth has won the argument. First, however, she bolsters his spirit; then reveals the method of the murder.

7. Macbeth is stunned. He applauds her courage, and briefly analyzes her plot.

8. Lady Macbeth confirms the plan, embellishing it with a show of cunning.

9. "I am settled," says Macbeth, inadvertently demonstrating how much swifter his wife is in action than he himself. "False face must hide what the false heart doth know." (Which is what his own wife has been saying since the beginning of the deadly enterprise.)

In this fifty-three-line exchange, Shakespeare orchestrates the conflict with a series of *rising emotional steps, or beats, which lead to a resolution of character and plot.*

What does this tell us about the process of revealing character?

1. *Character is revealed through conflict.*
2. *Conflict produces emotional heat.*
3. *The heat serves as rhythmic fuel to the event.*

The more that character becomes inseparable from event, the richer and more compelling is the conflict, and therefore the richer the experience is for reader and/or audience.

But let's not keep the Lady waiting:

II,ii: (*A WOMAN OF ACTION*)

At the end of II,i, Macbeth says,

> The bell invites me.
> Hear it not, Duncan, for it is a knell
> That summons thee to heaven, or to hell."

The next scene begins with Lady Macbeth entering from "hell."

LADY MACBETH
>That which hath made them drunk hath made me bold;
>What hath quenched them hath given me fire. Hark! Peace!
>It was the owl that shrieked, the fatal bellman
>Which gives the stern'st good-night. He is about it.
>The doors are open, and the surfeited grooms
>Do mock their charge with snores. I have drugged their possets.
>That death and nature do contend about them
>Whether they live or die.

MACBETH (*Within*)   Who's there? What, ho?

LADY MACBETH
Alack, I am afraid they have awaked,
And 'tis not done: the attempt, and not the deed,
Confounds us. Hark! I laid their daggers ready—
He could not miss 'em. Had he not resembled
My father as he slept, I had done't.
[*Enter* MACBETH.]   My husband!

MACBETH
I have done the deed. Didst thou not hear a noise?

LADY MACBETH
I heard the owl scream and the crickets cry.
Did not you speak?

MACBETH   When?

LADY MACBETH   Now.

MACBETH   As I descended?

LADY MACBETH   Ay.

MACBETH   Hark!
Who lies i' th' second chamber?

LADY MACBETH
Donalbain.

MACBETH
This is a sorry sight.

LADY MACBETH
A foolish thought, to say a sorry sight.

MACBETH
There's one did laugh in's sleep, and one cried "Murder!"
That they did wake each other. I stood and heard them.
But they did say their prayers and addressed them
Again to sleep.

LADY MACBETH
There are two lodged together.

MACBETH
One cried "God bless us!"

LADY MACBETH   Consider it not so deeply.

MACBETH
But wherefore could not I pronounce "Amen"?

I had most need of blessing, and "Amen"
Stuck in my throat.

LADY MACBETH
These deeds must not be thought
After these ways; so, it will make us mad.

MACBETH
Methought I heard a voice cry "Sleep no more!
Macbeth does murder sleep"—the innocent sleep,
Sleep that knits up the ravelled sleave of care,
The death of each day's life, sore labor's bath,
Balm of hurt minds, great nature's second course,
Chief nourisher in life's feast.

LADY MACBETH
What do you mean?

MACBETH
Still it cried "Sleep no more!" to all the house;
"Glamis hath murdered sleep, and therefore Caw-
    dor
Shall sleep no more, Macbeth shall sleep no more."

LADY MACBETH
Who was it that thus cried? Why, worthy Thane,
You do unbend your noble strength to think
So brainsickly of things. Go get some water
And wash this filthy witness from your hand.
Why did you bring these daggers from the place?
They must lie there: go carry them and smear
The sleepy grooms with blood.

MACBETH   I'll go no more.
I am afraid to think what I have done;
Look on't again I dare not.

LADY MACBETH   Infirm of purpose!
Give me the daggers. The sleeping and the dead
Are but as pictures. 'Tis the eye of childhood
That fears a painted devil. If he do bleed,
I'll gild the faces of the grooms withal,
For it must seem their guilt.

                              [*Exit.*]

A monstrous moment and—since now we must move
from the deed to examine its construction—an exciting

group of unintentional, prophetic utterances by both the Lady and her husband!

From the two-thirds' quoted scene, we learn that:

1. Lady Macbeth has left the grooms' daggers ready for Macbeth;
2. Macbeth has killed Duncan;
3. Because her husband is so shaken by the deed, the Lady herself has gone to plant the evidence—a pair of bloody knives—upon the grooms.

By playing the murder off-stage, Shakespeare allows us *to focus upon the characters' responses*, forcing us to witness the extent of their humanity. A lesser dramatist would have shown us the murder. Its horror would have made us turn away from the pair with disgust, revulsion and, most important, *with thorough emotional disengagement*.

The three *events* of the first two-thirds of this scene therefore have less to do with the physical murder *than with the psychological response* of the characters to the event.

Now examine the emotional beats—the growing heat—of the scene:

1. Lady Macbeth enters, drunk on the very boldness of their enterprise. When she hears a cry, she is startled. She fears Macbeth has bungled the murder. He appears.
2. But no, Macbeth has done the deed, and now begins to hallucinate. His conscience has gone on the attack. Desperately he has "most need of blessing."
3. Lady Macbeth tries to comfort him. (Unwittingly prophesying the very thoughts and voices that will drive the both of them mad.)
4. Macbeth's fears become more specific: he'd heard a voice cry "Sleep no more!" Where did the voice originate? From his conscience? The witches? Those agencies of darkness? We are prepared to accept *any possibility* at this point. Lady Macbeth doesn't

understand. Macbeth explains that he has heard that "Glamis-Cawdor-Macbeth shall sleep no more."

5. Again the Lady tries to calm his fears. Again, unwittingly she describes what later we will see when she herself has gone mad:

> Go get some water
> and wash this filthy witness from your hand.

Lady Macbeth tries to move her husband to action, where he will cease to think, where his guilts will not collapse upon him. But he is too frightened to confront his deed. Lady Macbeth takes the bloody daggers, and exits.

6. Immediately there is a knocking. And since we have accepted the existence of the witches, and have heard Macbeth paraphrase their behavior into his own fears, *anyone or any agency* now may enter the castle.

Thus Shakespeare *not only resolves* Duncan's murder in this scene, *but also prepares* for Macbeth's conscience to drive him to madness, and Lady Macbeth's activity to destroy her sanity.

Macbeth has been in a fever throughout these scenes. It is Lady Macbeth who, though possessed, has acted clearly. (Strangely enough, and paradoxically, Macbeth already is closer to health at this point than his own wife.)

    [*Knock Within*]
MACBETH
    Whence is that knocking?
    How is't with me when every noise appals me?
    What hands are here? Ha! they pluck out mine
        eyes.
    Will great Neptune's ocean wash this blood
    Clean from my hand? No, this my hand will
        rather
    The multitudinous seas incarnadine,
    Making the green one red.
        [*Enter* LADY MACBETH.]

LADY MACBETH
>My hands are of your color, but I shame
>To wear a heart so white. [*Knock*] I hear a
>>knocking
>
>At the south entry. Retire we to our chamber.
>A little water clears us of this deed.
>How easy is it then! Your constancy
>Hath left you unattended.
>>[*Knock*]   Hark! more knocking.
>
>Get on your nightgown, lest occasion call us
>And show us to be watchers. Be not lost
>So poorly in your thoughts.

MACBETH
>To know my deed, 'twere best not know myself.
>>[*Knock*]
>
>Wake Duncan with thy knocking! I would thou
>couldst.

>>>>>>>*[Exeunt.]*

By the end of the scene, Macbeth is in a state of fearful anxiety.

Again, by not traveling with Lady Macbeth to the scene of the crime, Shakespeare lets us concentrate on Macbeth's emotional dissolution; his fear of the knocking; his visual and psychic dislocation; his massive guilt. A soldier who can unfix a man "from nave to chops" is used to butchery: but regicide is a horror, as is the ultimate service of one's ambitions.

Lady Macbeth is active in the scene, supporting her husband, trying to allay his fears, then moving herself to perform when her husband no longer can act.

Although she becomes, in this last beat, the more decisive of the pair, and the more ghoulish ("Had he not resembled my father as he slept, I had done't"), note how Shakespeare's manipulation of Macbeth's conscience keeps the focus upon *him*, rather than upon his *wife*. Macbeth's cry at the end of the scene is a fatal attempt to redeem his own humanity to himself and to us:

Wake Duncan with thy knocking! I would thou couldst!

III,iii: ("*LOOK TO THE LADY*")

This complete scene plays approximately seven minutes. And in that time there are *fourteen* entrances, and *four* exits.

Macbeth himself appears and leaves the stage three times.

It is pure action now, for the characters have set the dreadful events in motion. The discovery of the murder is intended to be performed in a desperate frenzy:

> [*Bell rings. Enter* LADY MACBETH.]
> **LADY MACBETH**
> What's the business,
> That such a hideous trumpet calls to parley
> The sleepers of the house? Speak, speak!
> **MACDUFF**   O gentle lady,
> 'Tis not for you to hear what I can speak:
> The repetition in a woman's ear
> Would murder as it fell.
>   [*Enter* BANQUO.]   O Banquo, Banquo,
> Our royal master's murdered!
> **LADY MACBETH**   Woe, alas!
> What, in our house?

Macbeth is at his most active and imperious before his guests:

> **MACBETH**
> Had I but died an hour before this chance,
> I had lived a blessed time; for from this instant
> There's nothing serious in mortality:
> All is but toys. Renown and grace is dead,
> The wine of life is drawn, and the mere lees
> Is left this vault to brag of.

He admits to murdering the grooms, since he lies that they'd performed the regicide:

MACBETH
> Who can be wise, amazed, temp'rate and furious,
> Loyal and neutral, in a moment? No man.
> The expedition of my violent love
> Outrun the pauser, reason. Here lay Duncan,
> His silver skin laced with his golden blood;
> And his gashed stabs looked like a breach in
>   nature
> For ruin's wasteful entrance: there, the murderers,
> Steeped in the colors of their trade, their daggers
> Unmannerly breeched with gore. Who could
>   refrain
> That had a heart to love, and in that heart
> Courage to make's love known?

LADY MACBETH
> Help me hence, ho!

MACDUFF
> Look to the lady.

If Macbeth's aria of death and redemption is not sufficiently guileful and deceptive, Lady Macbeth's swoon seals the lie.

All is action.

We are shaken by the hypocrisy of the event, which now is fully reflected in the characters. Macbeth's line "There's nothing serious in mortality" will return to haunt him when "tomorrow, and tomorrow, and tomorrow, creeps in this petty pace..."

But the rules have changed.

Banquo later will ask: "Thou hast it now—King, Cawdor, Glamis, all."

But what about Banquo himself, who should be "the root and father of many kings?"

In that time, between the murder of Duncan and the discovery of his corpse, Macbeth has changed: his conscience seems to have been buried, and *the face of the savage warrior-king emerges*. If Banquo is to beget kings, though he be none, then Banquo must be killed as well.

MACBETH
> Here's our chief guest.

LADY MACBETH
> If he had been forgotten,
> It had been as a gap in our great feast,
> And all-thing unbecoming.

MACBETH
> To-night we hold a solemn supper, sir,
> And I'll request your presence.

Macbeth is as noble-sounding as his previous victim, and the Lady poisonously regal. Courtesy is an abstraction, for by now we are conditioned to assume the worst of motives from the soon-to-become royal couple.

Note the movement of Lady Macbeth in a few short scenes: from a solitary wife awaiting her husband's return from the wars, to the stately queen. But where is the real woman hidden?

Macbeth has dispatched two murderers to kill both Banquo and his son. Now he will attempt to deny prophecy itself.

This is another expository scene, full of preparatory moves. Note how Shakespeare alludes to: the death of Banquo; the further tormentings of Macbeth's conscience; the latter's sense that there may be no end to the murder before there is peace.

It is a brief view into the eye of Macbeth's haunted hurricane. (And the dramatists' art of *preparation*.)

Clearly this is Macbeth's scene.

The Lady is used as a foil for his plotting and imaginings. And yet Shakespeare does not write her woodenly, or leave her standing like a female Mister Interlocutor:

III,ii: (*A GOOD QUEEN, AND DOMESTIC*)

[*Enter* MACBETH's LADY *and a* SERVANT.]
LADY MACBETH
> Is Banquo gone from court?

SERVANT
> Ay, madam, but returns again to-night.

LADY MACBETH
Say to the King I would attend his leisure
For a few words.
SERVANT   Madam, I will.   [*Exit*.]
LADY MACBETH
Naught's had, all's spent,
Where our desire is got without content.
'Tis safer to be that which we destroy
Than by destruction dwell in doubtful joy.
          [*Enter* MACBETH.]
How now, my lord? Why do you keep alone,
Of sorriest fancies your companions making,
Using those thoughts which should indeed have died
With them they think on? Things without all remedy
Should be without regard. What's done is done.
MACBETH
We have scorched the snake, not killed it.
She'll close and be herself, whilst our poor malice
Remains in danger of her former tooth.
But let the frame of things disjoint, both the world suffer,
Ere we will eat our meal in fear, and sleep
In the affliction of these terrible dreams
That shake us nightly. Better be with the dead,
Whom we, to gain our peace, have sent to peace,
Than on the torture of the mind to lie
In restless ecstasy. Duncan is in his grave;
After life's fitful fever he sleeps well.
Treason has done his worst: nor steel nor poison,
Malice domestic, foreign levy, nothing,
Can touch him further.
LADY MACBETH   Come on.
Gentle my lord, sleek o'er your rugged looks;
Be bright and jovial among your guests to-night.
MACBETH
So shall I, love; and so, I pray, be you.
Let your remembrance apply to Banquo;
Present him eminence both with eye and tongue:
Unsafe the while, that we must lave

> Our honors in these flattering streams
> And make our faces vizards to our hearts,
> Disguising what they are.

LADY MACBETH   You must leave this.

MACBETH
> O, full of scorpions is my mind, dear wife!
> Thou know'st that Banquo, and Fleance, lives.

LADY MACBETH
> But in them Nature's copy's not eterne.

MACBETH
> There's comfort yet; they are assailable.
> Then be thou jocund. Ere the bat hath flown
> His cloistered flight, ere to black Hecate's summons
> The shard-borne beetle with his drowsy hums
> Hath run night's yawning peal, there shall be done
> A deed of dreadful note.

LADY MACBETH
> What's to be done?

MACBETH
> Be innocent of the knowledge, dearest chuck,
> Till thou applaud the deed. Come, seeling night,
> Scarf up the tender eye of pitiful day,
> And with thy bloody and invisible hand
> Cancel and tear to pieces that great bond
> Which keeps me pale. Light thickens, and the crow
> Makes wing to th' rooky wood.
> Good things of day begin to droop and drowse,
> Whiles night's black agents to their preys do rouse.
> Thou marvell'st at my words, but hold thee still;
> Things bad begun make strong themselves by ill.
> So prithee go with me.   [*Exeunt.*]

Though not advised of Macbeth's plot to kill his former companion-in-arms, Lady Macbeth's thoughts have begun to move in that direction. In four lines, Shakespeare poses the woman's uncertainty.

But as soon as Macbeth enters, she shakes off her own concerns.

> Things without all remedy
> should be without regard. What's done is done.

As Macbeth toils with his conscience, Lady Macbeth attempts to comfort him, to remove the scorpions plaguing his mind. Yet Macbeth no longer seems to need the woman's urgings to spur him to murder.

Note that as Macbeth rolls *with his own momentum*, the wife begins to sense this, and soon will come apart. What brought them together in an unholy pact no longer needs fierce coupling.

Subtly, *Shakespeare begins to reverse the roles:* Lady Macbeth attempts to be as reasonable as Macbeth in the first act. Macbeth, on the other hand, begins to invoke the same agencies of Evil as the Lady herself had done in I,v: his lines

> Come, seeling night,
> scarf up the tender eye of pitiful day

horribly and *deliberately* resembles the Lady's "Come, you spirits . . . unsex me here." The undoing of Macbeth, and the isolation and loneliness of his spouse commences at this scene.

How does Shakespeare accomplish this? Through role reversal and, paradoxically, uncoupling.

In this next scene, everything will begin to dissolve. While the Royal Guests wait at the table, Macbeth attends to Banquo's murderer:

III,iv: *(THE FALLING APART)*

MACBETH
There's blood upon thy face.
MURDERER   'Tis Banquo's then.
MACBETH
'Tis better thee without than he within.
Is he dispatched?
MURDERER   My lord, his throat is cut:
That I did for him.
MACBETH   Thou are the best o' th'
cut-throats.

> Yet he's good that did the like for Fleance:
> If thou didst it, thou art the nonpareil.

MURDERER
> Most royal sir, Fleance is 'scaped.

MACBETH [*Aside*]
> Then comes my fit again. I had else been perfect;
> Whole as the marble, founded as the rock,
> As broad and general as the casing air.
> But now I am cabined, cribbed, confined, bound in
> To saucy doubts and fears.—But Banquo's safe?

MURDERER
> Ay, my good lord. Safe in a ditch he bides,
> With twenty trenched gashes on his head,
> The least a death to nature.

MACBETH [*Aside*]   Thanks for that.
> There the grown serpent lies; the worm that's fled
> Hath nature that in time will venom breed,
> No teeth for th' present.—Get thee gone. To-morrow
> We'll hear ourselves again. [*Exit* MURDERER.]

LADY MACBETH
> My royal lord,
> You do not give the cheer. The feast is sold
> That is not often vouched, while 'tis a-making,
> 'Tis given with welcome. To feed were best at home;
> From thence, the sauce to meat is ceremony:
> Meeting were bare without it . . .

This is the very midpoint of the play.

Lady Macbeth, courteous as always, speaks two lines which are both hypocritical and yet pathetic:

> Pronounce (the welcome) for me, sir, to all our friends,
> For my heart speaks they are welcome.

A truth, and yet a lie.

Lady Macbeth's responses, both dark and pure, have

always been heartfelt. And now it will be her very heart that breaks.

Moreover, after Macbeth's asides with the Murderer, the Lady insists he give the toast of welcome, attempting to raise the tone of dinner to conviviality and love. Her attempt is all the more pathetic, for immediately Shakespeare undercuts the moment by bringing Banquo's ghost onstage. (By now, since we accept witches, we certainly will accept ghosts.)

Note how the scene builds in intensity:

> **LENNOX** May't please your Highness, sit.
> **MACBETH**
> Here had we now our country's honor roofed
> Were the graced person of our Banquo present—
> Who may I rather challenge for unkindness
> Than pity for mischance!
> **ROSS** His absence, sir,
> Lays blame upon his promise. Please't your Highness
> To grace us with your royal company?
> **MACBETH**
> The table's full.
> **LENNOX** Here is a place reserved, sir.
> **MACBETH**
> Where?
> **LENNOX**
> Here, my good lord. What is't that moves your Highness?

For Macbeth is convinced he is seeing Banquo's ghost. He rages:

> **MACBETH**
> Which of you have done this?
> **LORDS** What, my good lord?
> **MACBETH**
> Thou canst not say I did it. Never shake
> Thy gory locks at me.

ROSS
> Gentlemen, rise. His Highness is not well.

LADY MACBETH
> Sit, worthy friends. My lord is often thus,
> And hath been from his youth. Pray you keep
> seat.
> The fit is momentary; upon a thought
> He will again be well. If much you note him,
> You shall offend him and extend his passion.
> Feed, and regard him not.—Are you a man?

MACBETH
> Ay, and a bold one, that dare look on that
> Which might appal the devil.

LADY MACBETH
> O proper stuff!
> This is the very painting of your fear.
> This is the air-drawn dagger which you said
> Led you to Duncan. O, these flaws and starts
> (Imposters to true fear) would well become
> A woman's story at a winter's fire,
> Authorized by her grandam. Shame itself!
> Why do you make such faces? When all's done,
> You look but on a stool.

MACBETH   Prithee see there!
> Behold! Look! Lo! —How say you?
> Why, what care I? If thou canst nod, speak too.
> If charnel houses and our graves must send
> Those that we bury back, our monuments
> Shall be the maws of kites.   [*Exit* GHOST.]

LADY MACBETH
> What, quite unmanned in folly?

MACBETH
> If I stand here, I saw him.

LADY MACBETH
> Fie, for shame!

MACBETH
> Blood hath been shed ere now, i' th' olden time,
> Ere humane statute purged the gentle weal'
> Ay, and since too, murders have been performed
> Too terrible for the ear. The time has been

That, when the brains were out, the man would
die,
And there an end. But now they rise again,
With twenty mortal murders on their crowns,
And push us from our stools. This is more strange
Than such a murder is.

LADY MACBETH
My worthy lord,
Your noble friends do lack you.

MACBETH   I do forget.
Do not muse at me, my most worthy friends:
I have a strange infirmity, which is nothing
To those that know me. Come, love and health to
all!
Then I'll sit down. Give me some wine, fill full.

The forty-nine lines of this portion of the scene are a
fine example of Shakespeare's art: there are five distinct
emotional beats, which create a rich, rhythmical heat to
the drama:

1. Macbeth's toast.
2. His discovery of Banquo's Ghost.
3. The surprise of his guests, and Lady Macbeth's
   attempt to allay his fears.
4. The confrontation between the Lady and her
   husband.
5. Macbeth's slow return to the table, shaking off his
   "fit."

From Lady Macbeth's point-of-view, the scene is as
embarrassing as it is terrible. When Macbeth discovers
the ghost in his own place and challenges: "Which of you
have done this?" then screams at the ghost, "Thou canst
not say *I* did it," his confusion ("you have done this," "I
did it") is registered *vocally* as well as *visually*.

Ross's order to leave the table is topped by the Lady,
who begins to "vamp" until she can decide what to do. A
brilliant stroke of character, for Shakespeare has her order
the men to sit, then describes Macbeth's state to them;
then she tells the guests to ignore him, thereby giving

herself time to pull her husband away from the others and hiss: "Are you a man?"

Again, Lady Macbeth attempts to hit him where indeed it hurts, inveighing against his "flaws and starts," shaking him back to what she conceives to be the reality of the moment. But Macbeth is not "unmanned in folly." A ghost is a ghost, a witch is a witch. They were there. He saw them. He is seeing a ghost even now.

Everything is topsy-turvy, foul-fair.

Finally, growing more fearful that others will notice and will hear his folly, the Lady tries to bring her man back to social occasion.

Your noble friends do lack you.

This sequence of events is feverish, reaches its peak, and settles as Macbeth returns to the table.

But Shakespeare has not finished with him. *Once again* the Ghost appears.

[*Enter* GHOST.]

MACBETH
    I drink to th' general joy o' th' whole table,
    And to our dear friend Banquo, whom we miss.
    Would he were here! To all, and him, we thirst,
    And all to all.
LORDS   Our duties, and the pledge.
MACBETH
    Avaunt, and quit my sight! Let the earth hide
      thee!
    Thy bones are marrowless, thy blood is cold;
    Thou hast no speculation in those eyes
    Which thou dost glare with!
LADY MACBETH
    Think of this, good peers,
    But as a thing of custom. 'Tis no other.
    Only it spoils the pleasure of the time.
MACBETH
    What man dare, I dare.
    Approach thou like the rugged Russian bear,

The armed rhinoceros, or th' Hyrcan tiger;
Take any shape but that, and my firm nerves
Shall never tremble. Or be alive again
And dare me to the desert with thy sword.
If trembling I inhabit then, protest me
The baby of a girl. Hence, horrible shadow!
Unreal mock'ry, hence!   [*Exit* GHOST.]
                    Why, so; being gone,
I am a man again. Pray you sit still.

LADY MACBETH

You have displaced the mirth, broke the good
    meeting
With most admired disorder.

MACBETH   Can such things be,

And overcome us like a summer's cloud
Without our special wonder? You make me strange
Even to the disposition that I owe,
When now I think you can behold such sights
And keep the natural ruby of your cheeks
When mine is blanched with fear.

ROSS   What sights, my lord?

LADY MACBETH

I pray you speak not: he grows worse and worse;
Question enrages him. At once, good night.
Stand not upon the order of your going,
But go at once.

LENNOX   Good night and better health

Attend his Majesty.

LADY MACBETH

A kind good night to all.

                    [*Exeunt* LORDS.]

Lady Macbeth's excuse to the lords is pitiful, and now
Shakespeare paints her clearly unable to help her husband.
His ragings are now in the open, his thrashing at the
Ghost witnessed by all. In one moment he turns on his
own wife:

When I think you can behold such sights,
And keep the natural ruby of your cheeks

we are reminded of the extent of her own complicity.

Shakespeare has Ross interrupt this immediately, which stops Macbeth speaking personally against his wife (domestic quarrels in public—but from what a hideous frame of reference!).

Ross unwittingly asks Macbeth to state what he sees.

Instantly Lady Macbeth jumps in, unceremoniously dismissing the company.

All leave. The dinner has been a rout.

The focus now is fully upon Macbeth's emotional state, the pause inevitable before his speech. And this is the most interesting conclusion to the scene: Macbeth, alone again, recovers his sanity.

MACBETH
> It will have blood, they say: blood will have blood.
> Stones have been known to move and trees to speak;
> Augures and understood relations have
> By maggot-pies and choughs and rooks brought forth
> The secret'st man of blood. What is the night?

LADY MACBETH
> Almost at odds with morning, which is which.

MACBETH
> How say'st thou, that Macduff denies his person
> At our great bidding?

LADY MACBETH   Did you send to him, sir?

MACBETH
> I hear it by the way; but I will send.
> There's not a one of them but in his house
> I keep a servant fee'd. I will to-morrow
> (And betimes I will) to the weird sisters.
> More shall they speak, for now I am bent to know
> By the worst means the worst. For mine own good
> All causes shall give way. I am in blood
> Stepped in so far that, should I wade no more,

> Returning were as tedious as go o'er.
> Strange things I have in head, that will to hand,
> Which must be acted ere they may be scanned.

LADY MACBETH
> You lack the season of all natures, sleep.

MACBETH
> Come, we'll to sleep. My strange and self-abuse
> Is the initiate fear that wants hard use.
> We are yet but young in deed.

The critical moment has passed.

Expecting some horrible revelation, we are presented instead with *preparation for further development*. We listen attentively, because the emotional beats have been orchestrated with such intensity we fear that Macbeth, in his vision of the Ghost, may tell everything.

In these last lines, what expository preparations has Shakespeare planted?

1. Trees have been known to speak. (Now Macbeth himself is unconsciously prophesying his own death.)
2. Fair will remain foul.
3. MacDuff has refused to come to Macbeth, so there will be a showdown.
4. Macbeth will visit the witches again.

At this point Macbeth realizes that it is as difficult to return to innocence as it is to plough ahead in blood. He might as well move forward.

Lady Macbeth, while at first controlling the situation with remarkable aplomb, no longer can control the actions of her husband. *Her active role has ended*, her soul no longer needed to supply malignant energy to her husband's ambitions. All she can do now is listen to his plotting, offer solace, and slowly drown in her own poisons.

Unwittingly she repeats the words of the voices her husband had heard, after Duncan's murder in II,ii:

> You lack the season of all natures, sleep.

In these words, perhaps, we hear the echoes of her own restless giving-up.

V,i: *(A WALKER IN HELL)*
A full act has passed. The forces of MacDuff and Ross have rallied behind Duncan's son. The battle with Macbeth is inevitable.

There has been no reference to Lady Macbeth at all.

This scene, therefore, comes as a dramatic shock, at once surprising in its placement, and both pitiful and awesome in its execution.

[*Enter a* DOCTOR OF PHYSIC
and a WAITING GENTLEWOMAN.]

DOCTOR
I have two nights watched with you, but can perceive no truth in your report. When was it she last walked?

GENTLEWOMAN
Since his Majesty went into the field I have seen her rise from her bed, throw her nightgown upon her, unlock her closet, take forth paper, fold it, write upon't, read it, afterwards seal it, and again return to bed; yet all this while in a most fast sleep.

DOCTOR
A great perturbation in nature, to receive at once the benefit of sleep and do the effects of watching! In this slumb'ry agitation, besides her walking and other actual performances, what (at any time) have you heard her say?

GENTLEWOMAN
That, sir, which I will not report after her.

DOCTOR
You may to me, and 'tis most meet you should.

GENTLEWOMAN
Neither to you nor any one, having no witness to confirm my speech.

[*Enter* LADY MACBETH *with a taper.*]

In a lonely room in a castle, a lady is about to appear—once again, alone. Her solitude is profound. Note Shakespeare's symmetry: this last view of Lady Macbeth is similar to our first view, save that the woman's mental state is as distant from sanity as Uranus is from the Sun.

But Shakespeare wants us to make certain we understand her condition and pity it. This he accomplishes *by framing her scene within the comments of the Doctor and Gentlewoman*. By a series of questions and responses relating to her condition, Shakespeare tells us not only *exactly what we should watch*, but also *how we should feel*.

Lady Macbeth has become a sleepwalker, the result of her "great perturbation in nature." (And what else is this but a psychic rendering of "fair is foul?")

She is also given to speaking while sleepwalking. We can only imagine what she says. As you read the rest of the scene, note how Shakespeare *shapes our response* to Lady Macbeth, through his use of the Gentlewoman and the Doctor.

GENTLEWOMAN
Lo you, here she comes! This is her very guise, and, upon my life, fast asleep! Observe her; stand close.

DOCTOR
How came she by that light?

GENTLEWOMAN
Why, it stood by her. She has light by her continually. 'Tis her command.

DOCTOR
You see her eyes are open.

GENTLEWOMAN
Ay, but their sense are shut.

DOCTOR
What is it she does now? Look how she rubs her hands.

GENTLEWOMAN
It is an accustomed action with her, to seem thus washing her hands. I have known her continue in this a quarter of an hour.

LADY MACBETH
    Yet here's a spot.
DOCTOR
    Hark, she speaks. I will set down what comes
    from her, to satisfy my remembrance the more
    strongly.

Clearly Lady Macbeth is in a desperate state.

Twenty-seven lines of dialogue are focused upon her condition, and ten of which even whispered in her presence.

The doctor forces us to concentrate upon her speech, when he says he will set it down for remembrance.

And, after a silence, all the tortures of her mind burst forth, raging:

LADY MACBETH
    Out, damned spot! Out, I say! One—two—why
    then 'tis time to do't. Hell is murky. Fie, my
    lord, fie! a soldier and afeard? What need we fear
    who knows it, when none can call our power to
    accompt? Yet who would have thought the old
    man to have had so much blood in him?
DOCTOR
    Do you mark that?
LADY MACBETH
    The Thane of Fife had a wife. Where is she now?
    What, will these hands ne'er be clean? No more
    o' that, my lord, no more o' that! You mar all with
    this starting.
DOCTOR
    Go to, go to! You have known what you should
    not.
GENTLEWOMAN
    She has spoke what she should not, I am sure
    of that. Heaven knows what she has known.

All the images and hallucinations of Lady Macbeth, jumbled and rhythmically compelling as they are, directly relate to the grim events of the play. Shakespeare has provided us with a *recitative* of bloody ambition, a *reprise* of those specific events leading to her breakdown: the

blood of Duncan and the grooms; Macbeth's fears; the
regicide cover-up; the death of Ross's family; the agonies
of her own conscience; and the pursuit of ghosts:

> **LADY MACBETH**
> Here's the smell of the blood still. All the per-
> fumes of Arabia will not sweeten this little hand.
> Oh, oh, oh!
> **DOCTOR**
> What a sigh is there! The heart is sorely charged.
> **GENTLEWOMAN**
> I would not have such a heart in my bosom for
> the dignity of the whole body.
> **DOCTOR**
> Well, well, well.
> **GENTLEWOMAN**
> Pray God it be, sir.
> **DOCTOR**
> This disease is beyond my practice. Yet I have
> known those which have walked in their sleep
> who have died holily in their beds.
> **LADY MACBETH**
> Wash your hands, put on your nightgown, look
> not so pale! I tell you yet again, Banquo's buried.
> He cannot come out on's grave.
> **DOCTOR**
> Even so?
> **LADY MACBETH**
> To bed, to bed! There's knocking at the gate.
> Come, come come, come, give me your hand!
> What's done cannot be undone. To bed, to bed,
> to bed!   [*Exeunt.*]

Lady Macbeth's cry of guilt, "All the perfumes of
Arabia will not sweeten this little hand" becomes the
poignant *summa* of her condition. Although she appears to
sleep, her agony-ridden conscience remains violently awake.
This too becomes the fulfillment of the voices Macbeth
himself had heard after Duncan's murder: "Macbeth will
sleep no more." Horrid transference to his wife, doomed
to sleepwalk and to be tormented by her memories!

The Doctor hints at possible redemption, perhaps a medicinal plant ("I have known those which have walked in their sleep who have died holily in their beds."), but immediately after this line, Shakespeare brings up Banquo's death. The full chorus of murderous ambitions and torturing ghosts are brought to horrid light. Clearly living in and out of these moments of death, Lady Macbeth hears the porters' knock, the gates of Hell, and repeats her line from the banquet scene of III,ii: "What's done is done."

Poignantly, *in her own mad state, she still is fearing for her husband's sanity.* Sleeping and yet awake, she walks with the shade of her husband, to bed.

DOCTOR
   Will she go now to bed?
GENTLEWOMAN
   Directly.
DOCTOR
   Foul whisp' rings are abroad. Unnatural deeds
   Do breed unnatural troubles. Infected minds
   To their deaf pillows will discharge their secrets.
   More needs she the divine than the physician.
   God, God forgive us all! Look after her;
   Remove from her the means of all annoyance,
   And still keep eyes upon her. So good night.
   My mind she has mated, and amazed my sight.
   I think, but dare not speak.
GENTLEWOMAN   Good night, good
   doctor.

                                        [*Exeunt.*]

What are we to feel towards this woman?

Shakespeare seems to want us to answer, as the Doctor: "God, God forgive us all!"

Lady Macbeth is still a human being, and the Doctor's cry of humanity, his urging for the Gentlewoman to "look after her" is the redemption of our own humanity, our sympathy towards a woman now grievously alone. The Gentlewoman's parting line is a whisper of remembrance for the more blessed portions of mankind's endeavors, "Good night, good doctor."

It is a sigh accompanying the fall of a Lady who had loved her husband, who had sacrificed her soul for his ambition, and who now must bear the full burden of that sacrifice.

In V,iii, two scenes later, we hear that Lady Macbeth's condition has worsened. Macbeth, in the midst of battle, learns from the Doctor of his wife's illness.

> **MACBETH** Cure her of that!
> Canst thou not minister to a mind diseased,
> Pluck from the memory a rooted sorrow,
> Raze out the written troubles of the brain,
> And with some sweet oblivious antidote
> Cleanse the stuffed bosom of that perilous stuff
> Which weighs upon the heart?

Two scenes later, still in the midst of the battle, the officer Seyton informs Macbeth, "The Queen, my lord, is dead." And with her death, the meaning of "their bloody business" hits Macbeth with all of its horror, its terrible, rasping absurdity.

> **MACBETH**
> She should have died hereafter:
> There would have been a time for such a word.
> To-morrow, and to-morrow, and to-morrow
> Creeps in this petty pace from day to day
> To the last syllable of recorded time,
> And all our yesterdays have lighted fools
> The way to dusty death. Out, out, brief candle!
> Life's but a walking shadow, a poor player
> That struts and frets his hour upon the stage
> And then is heard no more. It is a tale
> Told by an idiot, full of sound and fury,
> Signifying nothing.

And it is done.
Hopefully Lady Macbeth did indeed "die holily" in her sleep.

Characters are defined by their own deeds and words. By the deeds and words of others.

By slow revelation of events which casts a strong and relentless light upon the unfolding of their souls.

What is the most important writing lesson we might learn from a study of Lady Macbeth?

The woman's deeds are indistinguishable from the yearnings of her soul.

Each scene reveals another aspect of her character as she both influences her husband, is influenced by him and, finally, is deserted by him in the midst of a battle of their own design.

The narrative line is, outwardly, simple.

Thrilled by the witches' prophecy, Lady Macbeth actively allows a murky hell to take over her loving nature. She becomes a co-conspirator in the events, and helps plan the death of a King. As new Queen, she is bountiful, and wears the royal robes with grace. As wife, however, she has become frightened by her husband's "voices," his visions of terror. Too late. Her man proceeds in his plotting *without her*, trying to buttress his short reign with further murders. She begins to collapse. To grow into madness. To die.

Dramatic as it is, the arc is swift, economical, harmonious.

As I had stated earlier, Lady Macbeth is alone and vibrant when we first encounter her. When we last see her she is *even* more alone, and hopelessly insane. *The effectiveness of this symmetry lies in its very simplicity.*

How does Shakespeare move her from innocence to torment?

Lady Macbeth is characterized not only by her own words and deeds, but also by her husband's response to them and, of course, to her. She is dramatized further by other figures: by Duncan, Banquo and, most movingly, by the Doctor and Gentlewoman.

Thus, the central characters of a work not only define their world for an audience but also, as they create that world, are themselves defined by it.

Each major character is shot from your dreams like an arrow.

Good archer that you are, you know where the arrow will land.

Your art, however, which is the conscious joy of creating character, lies in *harmoniously tracing the arc of the arrow* as it moves towards its destination.

Once again, go to a movie.

Or reread other pieces of dramatic literature to see the trajectory of the arc, asking yourself:

1. How far has the character traveled?
2. Is that character the same at the end of the drama as he or she was at the beginning? If so, why? If not, *how* has he or she changed?
3. *How inseparable is the character from the event, and the world of which he or she forms a major part?*
4. Does the character's dramatic life depend upon the performer playing it? (If so, it's a cheat.)
5. Does the character's dramatic life depend upon strong action? (If so, is it to hide a weakly developed character?)

And here are two *extremely* profitable questions:

If you remove the events, will the character disappear? (If so, the character never existed; if not, the character's capable of *everything*.)

If you remove the character, do the events themselves still remain? (If so, there never was a character at all.)

> If Character's no different from Event—
> God Bless!—you've written with intent.
> If Action's all your character's about,
> You've given birth to just another lout.

Creating characters springs from your dreams, observations, reflections; then from hearing the characters speak.

The process of revealing characters consists in putting them into the world, and knowing how they will end, and what they will become in that world.

The art of characterization consists in the slow revelation of his or her nature—as he or she travels toward his or her inevitable destination.

Character is defined by quality of voice; by deeds; by the response of others, through deed and word, towards being; by the character's interaction with the world.

Great characters are memorable because, by being creations of your own humanity, they interact with the humanity of the audience, and soon become its own.

Thus far we have analyzed the greater parts of our magical equation:

Idea + Force + Form = Idea Realized.

We have discussed a process of approaching the screenplay form; the critical first ten minutes of playing time; elements of exposition; characterization. We have shown that good characterization creates or is created by the dramatic event, and thus becomes indistinguishable from the event itself.

Shakespeare's plays aside, think of the characters in *Front Page, On The Waterfront, Mister Roberts, Some Like It Hot, Philadelphia Story, Annie Hall, Paths of Glory, Network, Doctor Strangelove, Fannie and Alexander,* to name a few films whose characters *are* the comic/tragic/melodramatic blood of the event. Can you divorce the drama from their being, or their being from the event?

Now think of *Towering Inferno, Jaws, Rocky, Star Wars, Porky's, Blues Brothers.* What remains in your memory of these latter "blockbusters?" A burning building; a mechanical monster; a stuttering slob with a butcher's heart of gold; nostalgia for Saturday afternoon serials or Saturday nights "live;" a one-line gag which lasts for two hours.

Trust your characters to take you to the end.

As you would never think of manipulating a friend, do not manipulate your characters.

And now let me sum up all I have to say about *Narration*:

Narration springs from *Character*.

Rhythm and Style

Let us dispose of a modern cinematic myth or, at least, modify it to a less grandiose scale:

The style and rhythm of film is dependent upon the director. Film, as the pundits have noted, is a director's medium.

First: what is rhythm? It is the dramatic pulse of the film, the controlled speed of the unfolding of character and event.

Second: what is style? Style is the particular way of perceiving and, therefore, of narrating the events.

Here is an example of *rhythm*, from Woody Allen and Marshall Brickman's *Annie Hall*:

ALVY: It's me. Open up.

ANNIE: Oh.

ALVY: Are you okay? What's the matter?

ANNIE: There's a spider in the bathroom.

ALVY: What?

ANNIE: There's a big black spider in the bathroom.

ALVY: That's what you got me here for at three o'clock in the morning, 'cause there's a spider in the bathroom?

ANNIE: My God, I mean, you know how I am about insects. . . . I can't sleep with a live thing crawling around in the bathroom.

ALVY: (*Sighing*) I told you a thousand times you should always keep, uh, a lotta insect spray. You never know who's gonna crawl over. . . .

Alvy is a reactor, a man continually viewing the world in comic horror: "Are you okay What's the matter? What? That's what you got me here for?"

Annie is phobic, childlike, a thoroughly intuitive woman whose comic charm (and therefore rhythm) emerges from her attempt to appear rational and in control of herself.

The trading of lines *arises directly* from these strokes of characterization. The rhythm of the language *is a result* of their inner lives, of the way they view the world and respond to events. The repetition is not merely a device to set up gags. It's a goggle-eyed vision of a man with thick glasses, and a woman constantly getting dust in her contact lenses.

It's funny, but it also hurts.

Style, unlike rhythm, is the particular way of viewing, and therefore narrating, the events.

Here is an example, from Paddy Chayevsky's *Network:*

DIANA moves languidly to the door and would leave, but MAX suddenly says:

MAX: I don't get it, Diana. You hung around till half-past seven and came all the way down here just to pitch a couple of looney show biz ideas when you knew goddam well I'd laugh you out of the office. I don't get it. What's your scam in this anyway?

DIANA moves back to the desk and crushes her cigarette out in the desk tray.

DIANA: Max, my little visit here tonight was just a courtesy made out of respect for your stature

in the industry. . . . But sooner or later I'm
going to take over your network news show,
and I figured I might as well start tonight. . . .

She smiles, glides to the doorway again.

MAX: Listen, if we can get back for a moment to
that gypsy who predicted all that about
emotional involvements and middle-aged
men—what're you doing for dinner tonight?

DIANA pauses in the doorway, and then moves back
briskly to the desk, picks up the telephone receiver,
taps out a telephone number, waits for a moment—

DIANA: (*On phone*) I can't make it tonight, luv, call
me tomorrow.

She returns the receiver to its cradle, looks at MAX;
their eyes lock.

MAX: Do you have any favorite restaurant?

DIANA: I eat anything.

MAX: Son of a bitch, I get the feeling I'm being
made.

DIANA: You sure are.

MAX: I better warn you I don't do anything on the
first date.

DIANA: We'll see.

She moves to the door. MAX stares down at his desk.

MAX: (*Mutters*) Schmuck.

He sighs, stands, flicks off his desk lamp.

Since Diana is the more active in the scene, Chayevsky
favors Max's view of her: he watches her cross to the door,
then return, lean over the lamp. Stub out her cigarette in
the ashtray. Return to the door. Turn. Move to the telephone.
Place the call. Stare at Max. Leave. Then, to make sure
we know what Max is feeling, Chayevsky has him stare at
the desk and swear at himself.

The style is tight, tough, grimly comic—Chayevsky's
view of the woman is as a predator (Diana the Huntress);
of Max as a self-doubter attracted by her attractions, and
yet intelligent enough to know he is being had.

*Chayevsky's view of his characters sets the style of the
work. The voices of the characters themselves create the
rhythm.*

* * *

If a screenplay tells a story about a character who creates or is involved in an event, and so becomes indistinguishable from the event itself, a rhythm occurs, *which is the rhythm of the character himself; which is the way he battles the world, and either affects or is affected by the world*.

Admittedly, as subjective as this is, the *style of the work* should be both the result of the interaction of character and event and produced rhythm, *and also the way in which the writer perceives that interaction*.

However, this is not to say that style is something to be imposed upon the character or event. It emerges from the characters, and the author's own view of them.

It is better for a screenwriter to spend his time developing his characters than to worry about the "style" of the film. (This is the mononucleosis of cinéastes, the students' disease. How many young film-makers are involved in *"film noir,"* without ever having read Horace McCann, James M. Cain, Raymond Chandler, and without having understood the social realities from which those novels and stories were written—i.e., that the works emerged from reality, and not from "style" for its own sake?)

When style does emerge, hopefully it will be at the service of character and event, rather than at the mercy of the writer's own ego, or the bizarre variables of production.

By now it should be apparent to you that I care not a whit for the argument of form vs. content, for I am a lousy dualist.

Rather, I believe in the alchemy of our magical trine:

Idea + Force + Form = Idea Realized.

Your thoughts, words, dreams exist as tools to support the birth of a fictional being, who will move unselfconsciously (style), and at his own particular pace (rhythm).

Briefly:
Introduce a real character really into the world.

He or she will create the rhythm of that world as he or she learns to walk or to fly, to swim or to tango. The events in which your characters find themselves will suggest a manner of narration, or style. A warning is implied: *the more you impose yourself between the characters and public (through gifted prose, or glorious camera angles), the less chance the characters will have to survive.*

Two examples of this self-imposition:

Let us repeat the ANNIE HALL scene. But *let us comment* upon Annie while we are seeing it, imposing ourselves between the viewer and the characters:

> ANGLE OF ANNIE'S bedstand: cigarettes overflow in ashtrays, and a pile of books crowd the stand. WE READ the titles: *Color Me Beautiful;* Kennedy's *Profiles in Courage;* Jane Fonda's *Exercise Book;* Fulton Oursler's *The Greatest Story Ever Told.* Beside the books a radio blares: a talk show about How Difficult it is for Woman to Live in Man's World. OFF-CAMERA, WE HEAR:
>
> ALVY: It's me. Open up. [Etc.]

By imposing such details upon the viewer, we never give them a *chance to make up their own minds about Annie.* Instead, we tell them a great deal about her, without letting Annie show herself. Allen and Brickman, however, accomplish this detail a few lines later, when Alvy hands Annie a magazine with which to smash the spider. Suddenly he grabs the magazine from her, and stares at it:

> ALVY: What is this? Since when do you read the *National Review?* What are you turning into?
> ANNIE: Well, I like to get all points of view.
> ALVY: It's wonderful. Then why don'tcha get William F. Buckley to kill the spider?

In this scene of comic conflict, Annie's own confusions are delightfully *dramatized*, not told. And the writers let us *come to our own conclusion* about both Annie and Alvy.

Another example:

Suppose, in the *Network* scene, we were to revise the quoted scene to include the following:

> **DIANA:** (*On phone*) I can't make it tonight, luv, call me tomorrow.
>
> She returns the receiver to its cradle, looks at Max; their eyes lock.
>
> **MAX:** Have you really given a thought to infidelity, Diana? Don't you think it cheapens our lives?

Implied in this example are a series of no-nos:

Don't editorialize your characters. Let them be the stuff of their own lives.

Don't impose your own world-view *directly* upon them, for they don't know you. Rather, let them be *dramatized reflections* of your ethical sensibilities.

To modify the opening lines of this section:

Is the basic style and rhythm of the film dependent upon the director?

NO.

It is totally dependent upon you, the writer, and your own relationship to the characters.

A Few Lines About Dialogue

By now it should be apparent that the purpose of this book is to enable you to find a way to think about your characters, and to develop them skillfully. It assumes that people make the world move, even as the world moves people.

Dialogue, therefore, is central *to your own understanding* of your character, as well as to the audience's.

Dialogue is the spirit of the drama.

For me, writing dialogue is pleasure: the rhythms, tensions, word play, nuance make the very act of screenwriting a noisy, companionable affair.

Earlier I had mentioned that I cannot write until I hear my characters speak. I'll amend that: I *refuse to write* until they tell me who they are. I'm a pleasant fellow, and certainly don't force my company to speak if they don't wish.

I suggest you don't, either.

After a time, if your characters still don't speak, you might try an exercise through *negation:*

Ask yourself, If Silent Jennifer were to confront the ailing Mrs. Hanna, what would she say?

Even more specifically, if Silent Jennifer had to learn from Mrs. Hanna where she kept her will, how would she go about confronting the woman?

(Would she plead? Bargain? Pretend to be sweet? Perhaps she wouldn't say anything at all, and that might well be the key to Jennifer's character.)

Until you understand your character (and it may be an intuition, rather than an intellectual understanding), you will not know how he/she speaks. But once you *do* understand your character, the voice should move smoothly through his/her wiring, and into yours.

A horrible truth: *bad dialogue more often than not means bad characterization.*

Even if your dramatic situation is satirical, *good* dialogue instantly will create the universe you are satirizing.

What do we learn of the following characters?

MANDRAKE:	Excuse me, sir, something rather interesting's just cropped up. Listen to that—music, civilian broadcasting. Choc-a-bloc full of stations all churning it out.
RIPPER:	Mandrake?
MANDRAKE:	Yes, sir.

RIPPER:	I thought I issued instructions for all radios on this base to be impounded.
MANDRAKE:	Well, you did indeed, sir, and I was in the process of impounding this very one when I happened to switch it on—
RIPPER:	Group Captain. The Officer Exchange Programme does not give you any special prerogatives to question my orders.
MANDRAKE:	Well I, I realize that, sir, but I thought you'd be rather pleased to hear the news. After all, well, let's face it, we don't want to start a nuclear war unless we really have to, do we?

It's from the Stanley Kubrick-Terry Southern-Peter George screenplay of *Dr. Strangelove*.

From the scene quoted above, the reader can deduce that Ripper is, at the very least, a stickler for orders; that Mandrake is exceptionally polite and somewhat afraid of Ripper. The "let's face it" and "*really* have to" in the midst of Mandrake's last speech is a brilliant character touch, totally unmilitary, fearful, and marking time to see the extent of Ripper's dementia.

Does the dialogue reflect the characters' mental and emotional states?

If you closed your eyes and heard the dialogue, could you distinguish one character from another?

How is the dialogue related to the event? Does it advance the story, permit us to see into the characters' minds and hearts?

Here is another example that both defines character and moves the plot forward:

BIALYSTOCK:	Yes?
BLOOM:	Yes, what?
BIALYSTOCK:	What you were saying. Keep talking.
BLOOM:	What was I saying?

BIALYSTOCK: You were saying that under the right circumstances, a producer could make more money with a flop than he could with a hit.

BLOOM: Yes, it's quite possible.

BIALYSTOCK: You keep *saying* that, but you don't tell me how. . . .

BLOOM: It's simply a matter of creative accounting. Let us assume, just for the moment, that you are a dishonest man.

BIALYSTOCK: Assume away!

BLOOM: Well, it's very easy. You simply raise more money than you really need.

BIALYSTOCK: What do you mean?

BLOOM: You didn't go all the way. . . . You could have raised a million dollars, put on a sixty thousand dollar flop and kept the rest.

BIALYSTOCK: But what if the play was a *hit*?

BLOOM: Oh, you'd go to jail. . . .

BIALYSTOCK: Aha, aha, aha, aha, *aha*! So, in order for the scheme to work, we'd have to find a sure-fire flop.

BLOOM: What scheme?

BIALYSTOCK: What scheme? *Your* scheme, you bloody little genius!

BLOOM: Oh, no. No. No. I meant no scheme. I merely posed a little academic accounting theory. It's just a thought.

BIALYSTOCK: Bloom, worlds are turned on such thoughts!

Mel Brooks's brilliant exposition serves not only to define his larcenous universe, but also to show us his heroes' mental and emotional workings. Bloom is a quiet dreamer; Bialystock, an energetic thief. Together they create *The Producers*, one of the most outrageous American comedies of the last thirty years.

* * *

Many film critics, and a great deal of screenplay literature, will tell you that an image will suffice, rather than a page of dialogue.

If the image allows you to explore the inner life of your characters, this certainly may be true.

But screenplays are still *plays*, and unless we revert to our ancestry (silent movies, and the planet of the apes), language will still be spoken.

And good language, whether spoken on stage or screen, is always a pleasure to hear.

Because good language means good characterization.

Part Three:

Writing Adaptations

Adapting works from another medium is an excellent exercise in craft: not only must you satisfy the author's vision in dramatic and visual terms, but also you must satisfy the audience's preconceived attitudes towards the work—or at least give them the sense that they are viewing the film version of the source material.

With works of mass appeal, it is relatively simple to satisfy the audience. Most bestsellers rely upon action rather than upon characterization to tell the tale. Action, the easiest aspect of the screenplay to manipulate, carries an instant punch which is also the most forgettable. It is pure popcorn—hardly a memorable meal.

With works of literary stature, the problem becomes much more difficult: how to respect the author's vision, language, and themes without creating a work that moves at snail's pace, and lacks certain dramatic intensity. After all, the relationship between a novelist and his reader is much more intimate, leisurely, and allows the reader to review sections of the work, to pace his own reading from a variety of settings: bedroom, beach, bathroom, bus, and so on.

A dramatic work must pick up an anonymous mass *and move the audience as one* through a very specific landscape. At no time must it give the mass a moment to think, to comment or to complain—until after the drama has finished. If the audience stops during the drama to make comparisons between the book and the film, then the tension has been lost.

Over the years I have found certain guidelines to be effective:

Let's assume that you have accepted an assignment from a producer to adapt a certain novel. Therefore, you and the novel and the producer AND the audience are mutually committed. Here are three steps which you should follow, and which will define your own attitude towards the assignment.

Steps in Writing an Adaptation

1. *Read the Source Material.*
   Read the work for pleasure. Forget that you are about to adapt it for the screen. *What did you like best about the work? Why?*

2. *Now Reread the Novel, Asking Yourself:*
   A) What are the author's principal concerns, themes? *How does he convey them to the audience?*
   B) Who are the major characters? *How do they interact with the themes, the narrative?*
   C) What does the author wish our attitude to be towards his characters and themes? *How does he manipulate us to accomplish his end?*
   D) Does the narration advance theme and character? *If so, how?*

In other words, examine the work from within the text itself, the novelist's craft.

3. *Then Throw the Text Away, and Dream What You Have Absorbed As Film.*

BUT let us assume that the author cares as much about language as he does content.

This is where adapting can be fun.

Examine the author's style: his tone, rhythm, speech and narrative cadence; his use of metaphor or simile. Is it an integral part of the reading experience? Frequently, if the book is a bestseller, the language is pitiful, cliché-ridden, and serves only to move plot forward; the language is a garage-mechanic's tool, and every bit as oily.

But *if not*, how do you translate the author's style onto the screen?

The answer is as simple as the execution is not:

Make the author's language an integral part of character and plot.

Translating an Author's Literary Style to Film: One Example

Listen:

Billy Pilgrim has come unstuck in time.

Billy has gone to sleep a senile widower and awakened on his wedding day. He has walked through a door in 1955 and come out another one in 1941. He has gone back through that door to find himself in 1963. He has seen his birth and death many times, he says, and pays random visits to all the events in between.

He says.

Billy is spastic in time, has no control over where he is going next, and the trips aren't necessarily fun. He is in a constant state of stage fright, he says, because he never knows what part of his life he is going to have to act in next.

—Kurt Vonnegut, Jr. *Slaughterhouse Five*

At first, Vonnegut's style appears to be deliberately flat, unsentimental, with very little editorializing, or commenting upon characters. Then one begins to notice the cadence—spare, but punctuated with tight, jazzy riffs. The *simplicity* of the *language serves to understate* the events. It also hides a rather complex structure:

"Billy is spastic in time, has no control over where he is going next."

The book becomes seemingly spastic as well, a time-travel of Billy's life, his family, the values of a world which has served to deaden him. The language of each scene is deliberately bonepicked and gives the appearance of being "objective," without leavening.

The language of the film should therefore mirror Vonnegut's. It too should be spare, simple, understated. The movement of the film should mirror the unstrung quality of the book.

The *dialogue should also be* equally underwritten, in an almost Dick-and-Jane style, its characters becoming Vonnegut's own hidden commentary.

Billy, knowing the plane was going to crash pretty soon, closed his eyes, traveled in time back to 1944. He was back in the forest in Luxembourg again—with the Three Musketeers. Roland Weary was shaking him, bonking his head against a tree. "You guys go on without me," said Billy Pilgrim.

Therefore, in translating the language into scenes, the same spareness, flatness of narration (which serves to amplify the horror of the events) should be used. From my screenplay:

BILLY
That's my Mom. In our backyard.
DERBY studies the photograph.
DERBY
You have a very nice-looking mother.
BILLY
Well, yes, she is.
DERBY
Very nice. Nice house, too.

BILLY

That's the back.

DERBY

Nice yard. Nice.

This flatness becomes pathetic, ridiculous.

DRIVER

For God's sake, why'd you jam on your brakes!?

VALENCIA

My Billy fell from a plane.

The cliché is turned against itself, so the audience soon becomes aware of the same word play Vonnegut himself has used:

BILLY

I don't mean to be impolite . . . but how did *you* end up here?

DERBY

I'll tell you, son. I couldn't afford *not* to. Not while the Nazis and the Japanese were threatening to conquer the world. Matter of fact, I got a boy, about your age, seeing action in the South Pacific. . . .

BILLY

Gosh, that's really . . . *something*!

DERBY

(*Shrugging*)

Back home I used to tell my students: There's a monster loose in the world. I just got tired of tellin' 'em, and decided to do something about it.

BILLY

I *thought* you were a teacher! You have that confidence, and a very good way with words.

DERBY

Well, I tell you one thing: you don't mince phraseologies at Boston Trade and Industrial.

What I was attempting to do in the adaptation was to give *a sense of Vonnegut's style*, through dialogue and scene rhythm, written à la Vonnegut. I was deliberately dramatizing the scene *in the author's own style*. Much of the pleasure of the novel is Vonnegut's voice. And, without attempting a voice-over narration (which would have been even more eccentric than the story), I tried to *put his language* into an immediate, dramatic context. This would allow the audience to believe they were witnessing the novel (all of the time they were), *because they were hearing Vonnegut's voice* (most of the time they weren't).

After you have understood the meaning of the novel, and have analyzed the author's method of narration, you must attempt to find a dramatic equivalent of the author's style—to be used through dialogue and scene rhythm.

Scene Rhythm: More Examples from Slaughterhouse-Five

If Billy Pilgrim, the film's hero, becomes unstuck in time, then the film must do the same thing. Although Billy "has no control over where he is going next," the film must give that same impression *but all the while going somewhere*—otherwise it will end up as a random collection of scenes, presented randomly.

There is a logic to Billy's pilgrimage.

Every time he has said Yes to society, he has nearly drowned; or been taken prisoner by the enemy; or lost his wife; or died in a plane crash. When, finally, Billy says No, constructing his own prison on Tralfamadore (an emotional zig away from the book's zag), and decorating the zoo-prison with a mate of his choice, he can begin to come unstuck un/happily ever after. Within these events, therefore, a certain chronology can be constructed, from which the larger movement of the film will emerge:

World War II—Billy is taken prisoner, lives through the

horrors of Dresden, sees his only friend killed, and survives;

Post-World War II—Billy marries the boss's daughter, becomes a respected citizen, fathers two dreadful children, is the only survivor of an optometrists' flight to Montreal; loses his wife in an auto crash, his son to the Green Berets; is "abducted" by the Tralfamadorians.

On Tralfamadore—Billy lives with his new mate, Montana Wildhack, fathers a boy, and continues to come unstuck in time and space.

The three scene blocks—World War II, Post-WW II, and Tralfamadore—possess a definite rhythm and chronology, a beginning, middle, and an end.

Therefore, we can cut between these three parallel blocks, giving the audience the sense that the affair *is* random, but all the while *moving towards a definite conclusion*. Moreover, *we can comment upon the action without ever saying a word:* through the juxtaposition of the image at the end of one scene with the image at the beginning of the next. Remember? Cutting between scenes?

How is this accomplished?

A few examples:

Slaughterhouse Five begins with Billy writing a letter to the editor of the local paper, stating that he has come unstuck in time:

". . . That is to say, I might go to sleep right in 1972, and wake up back in World War II. . . . It really isn't as much fun as it might sound. Mostly because I have no control over it, so I don't know what part of my life I'm going to end up in next." (Remember about *stating the physical conventions of the film in its first ten minutes?*)

Billy continues: "However there are compensations. Tralfamadore, for instance, as I explained in my last letter."

Immediately we cut to Montana Wildhack, Billy's zoo-mate, who is in a geodesic dome, humming and reading to herself. She looks at the camera as if it were Billy, smiles and winks.

Cut back to Billy's response. Still in his earth room, he smiles, returns the wink. In that gesture the unstucking is dramatized. Suddenly we hear a rumble. Billy's eyes grow wide.

Cut to a German half-rack running through a field in Belgium.

Then a shot of Billy's eyes again. But this time he is twenty years old, and lost in the war.

Billy meets up with his future murderer, the young Paul Lazzarro, in a ditch. All are lost. Billy, an assistant chaplain, begins to pray. Suddenly he is back on Tralfama-dore. Montana realizes he has been time-tripping, and attempts to comfort him.

> **MONTANA**
> How about a little kiss?
>> **BILLY**
>> A little kiss?
> (*Back in the ditch*, LAZZARRO *turns to* BILLY, *surprised*.)
>> **LAZZARRO**
>> What?
>> **BILLY** (*Eyes closed*)
>> A little kiss?
>> **LAZZARRO**
>> Goddamn! Goddamn fag...!
> (*He grabs his cock*.)
>> It's hard! The fag's gotta hard-on!

The time-tripping continues to plunge Billy into scenes of gloom or rapture, faithful to Vonnegut's vision, and all the time moving Billy's own development forward.

Psychological States Revealed Through Cutting Between Scenes: More Examples

How to show the psychological pilgrimage of Billy—through scenes of humiliation, fear, alienation, and panic? Watch the juxtaposition of images. The scenes themselves do not comment upon his state. The *images* do.

Humiliation

Marching to prison, Billy is chosen to be photographed by the Germans:

> TWO PHOTOGRAPHERS grab BILLY from the line and set him before a stationary motion picture camera. They cue several guards, who grab BILLY and push him into a bombed-out building that is mostly rubble. BILLY smiles at the guards, as the photographer shouts:

> **PHOTOGRAPHER**
> (*In German*)
> Go ahead!

> And the photographer slugs BILLY on the chin, sending him into the rubble as we:

> CUT TO:
> EXT. PILGRIM BUILDING—DAY—ANOTHER PHOTOGRAPHER—1958
> In front of the Pilgrim Building is an 8×10 still camera with flashbulbs. It is summer, 1958. BARBARA and ROBERT are 10 and 9. BILLY, holding a huge

pair of scissors to cut a tape; VALENCIA; Billy's father-in-law, LIONEL MERBLE, are posing for photographers in front of a new, modern Medical Building in Illium. Standing about in admiring groups are employees, other doctors, wives, etc. There is a large sign in evidence across the front of the building that says PILGRIM BUILDING. During all of the following, the photographers are posing the family group and giving them instructions to smile, etc., and several flat flash photographs are taken. These will be frozen after every flash, into black and white stills, and the dialogue will continue and be picked up again in action in color causing a straight jump cut.

Fear and Alienation
BILLY has tucked himself into a fetal position under the blanket. The sound of the hobo becomes muffled as BILLY pulls the blanket over his eyes, the boxcar door slams and

CUT TO:

INT. HOSPITAL ROOM—NIGHT
(DARKNESS [1946])

MOTHER'S VOICE
He was at the top of his class in
Optometry School when this happened.
ROSEWATER'S VOICE
I don't doubt it, Mrs. Pilgrim.

Underneath the covers of a hospital bed. One corner is slightly raised and, through it, we can see a hospital bedside table with the usual utensils, glass of water, vase of flowers, etc.

Sitting beside the bed is a benign and wrinkled apple who is Billy's mother. In the next bed is another patient, ELLIOT ROSEWATER, a large, intensely sympathetic man. They are both looking towards the small opening in the covers. The windows beyond are covered in mesh.

> **MOTHER**
> The doctor says it's a case of
> nervous exhaustion.

A Living Death
>   Weary's head falls back. He's dead.
>   In fear, BILLY moves back. LAZZARRO's eyes burn
> into him.

> **LAZZARRO**
>   Weary's dead, Pilgrim . . . !
>   BILLY closes his eyes.
>   INT. SHOCK ROOM OF A MENTAL HOSPITAL—
> DAY—1946
>   THE CAMERA looks straight down on a table on which
> BILLY lies, stretched out. We are also looking down
> on the tops of the heads of the DOCTOR and his
> assistants and a small group of interns who accompany
> him.

Total Regression, Fear, and Panic
>   BILLY and DERBY enter the shower among the
> other naked men. BILLY looks up to a shower head.
>   CUT TO:
>   INT. INDOOR POOL AND SHOWER—DAY—
> CLOSEUP SHOWER HEAD—1932
>   Water crashes out of the shower head, and WE PAN
> down to see a small naked boy, about eight, young
> BILLY PILGRIM. The water stops and he is scooped
> up by a large, hairy mustachioed man. The action is
> slightly sped up. In the background a gramophone
> plays a Rudy Vallee record.
>   The man, Billy's FATHER, carries him through a
> group of other pot-bellied men towards an indoor
> pool.

> **FATHER**
> Here we go, Billy!

>   The camera stays close on BILLY's terrified face, his
> eyes tightly shut. The other men shout their encour-
> agement.

OTHERS
(Ad lib)
That's the way to do it, Jim!
That's how I learned!
It'll make a man of him!
My father did it to me, believe me.
I *learned fast*, etc.

More laughter. Billy's FATHER reaches the end of the pool, and flings BILLY high into the air and into the pool.

FATHER
It's sink or swim, Billy, don't
forget to kick...

The UNDERWATER CAMERA PICKS him up; without a struggle, BILLY lets air out and sinks gently past the camera leaving a trail of air bubbles. the CAMERA TILTS up to a bright light above the pool, seen through the water. We HEAR "Links, recht, links, recht" as the camera tilts down from:

EXT. DETENTION CAMP—NIGHT—DETENTION CAMP STREET LIGHT—1944

We see the prisoners being led through the prison camp at night, being led by several guards.

In the above scenes, Billy's psychological state is commented upon by the contrast of *images linking scenes*.

Billy has become so psychologically reduced that when an English officer tells him how to survive the war and asks, "It's a matter of self-discipline and training, actually. Think you can do it?" Billy smiles politely, falls into his soup, and WE HEAR Billy say, voice-over, "Here, Spot."

EXT. BILLY'S HOUSE—DAY—1948

The screen is a pattern of summery colors which shift quickly, take form, and we are in a garden. We hear a dog barking. Shriller than the dog which had been with the German Patrol.

Camera arcs in air, following the flight of an object whirling through space. It falls to earth. A bone.

Dog barking grows louder. Spot, a cocker spaniel pup, enters the picture, seizes the bone, worries it, then scampers past Billy, who is dressed in flannels, carrying a rolled-up newspaper. Billy tries to smack the pup.

In the screenplay, Tralfamadore is introduced when Valencia humiliates Billy and Spot at a party for baby Barbara. Isolated from a rotten marriage (even when Billy does the "right thing," it backfires):

EXT. BILLY'S DOCK—NIGHT

Billy and Spot are seated on the dock, looking up at the Heavens. Billy is tremendously dejected. FROM BILLY'S POINT-OF-VIEW we see the sky. A shooting star blazes across, then seems to stop, and to reverse its direction.

Billy watches it, puzzled. From BILLY'S POINT-OF-VIEW it BEGINS to move closer to him. Billy holds Spot and rises. The dog begins to whine.

The star starts to move towards Billy slightly. A light starts to grow on Billy's and Spot's faces, as though a source of light was approaching them. They both stand very still, watching whatever it is. Then after a moment the light starts to recede.

Billy and Spot stare after it thoughtfully for a while, then turn and start slowly into the house.

And so it goes.

The use of image-juxtaposition to comment upon a

psychological state does not need as eccentric a format as *Slaughterhouse Five*.

It can work just as effectively in a chronological—or linear—plot.

Such a technique is a dynamic way to not only tell the tale, but also to reveal the inner state of the central figures—without boring the viewer by overtly commenting upon that state.

Remember: tricksters do not give away the secrets of their craft. While the audience is amazed by the first conjuring, the trickster is midway into the second.

As you can see, the process of writing adaptations is no different *in form* than the process of writing original works. Where the writer *legitimately must move away from the source material* is in the movement of scenes and, therefore, in the *timing* of character revelation.

A novelist may take thirty pages to make one dramatic point. In film *this same point* can be made in four lines. The setting of the visual stage, the atmosphere, the luxury of psychical surroundings can be established quickly in a montage, or through a series of juxtaposed images. As long as the atmosphere remains faithful to the book, *and the style is adequately translated,* then the scenes need *not follow the exact order of events* as written in the novel, play, or short story.

Character often is sketched in bestsellers, rather than developed. It is as if the author were "pitching" his story to a studio rather than telling it to a reader. Since the characters are little more than pawns, the screenwriter can "improve" upon the author's limited vision.

On the other hand, good writers create characters of subtlety and nuance.

The solution for the screenwriter is *to utilize the author's style and language in dramatic form, to give the equivalent visual sense of subtlety and depth*.

Often, however, the original dialogue is stylized, is meant to be read rather than acted. A performer playing Hemingway's dialogue, for example, would be laughed off the screen. Hemingway, who probably wrote the worst dialogue in the century (and which might tell us something about the depth of those characters speaking that dialogue) utilized repetitive, highly mannered, voice, which seemed more to be an extension of narrative atmosphere rather than concern for character.

To give the impression, however, that Hemingway is being *seen*, the screenwriter would have to create understated and terse characters, *always playable*, whose voices were not mannered and, therefore, offensive to the ears:

> "Is it good, Maria? Do you like the wine? Is it honest?"
> "Yes, John. It is an honest wine, and a good. I like it. I like the wine."
>
> —Arthur Hemingway, *The Son Also Told, The Bell's Also Rising*

Unless this exchange were played by arch comedians it would be embarrassing. But the *effect of this style* can be created by playing off the pauses, the unspoken tension between the two characters:

> **JOHN**
> Is it good, Maria?
>
> MARIA, from JOHN'S POV: *she looks up, calculatingly*.
>
> The wine?
>
> MARIA *smiles slightly, before answering*.
> **MARIA**
> It is . . . honest.

She watches John for the effect of her words.
He nods coolly, then drinks, glancing up at her.
She continues to smile.

The pauses became filled with (boorish) innuendo.
And because Maria cannot speak English very well, we are deliberately made to remain in a state of ambiguity about her sentiments. (As well as why we are in the

heater at all.) Yet we have a *sense* that those were the author's exact words.

Implied in this text is the idea that more often than not you will be asked to adapt clinkers.

This is not cynicism on my part. Most filmed adaptations are based on novels you wouldn't even take the time to read. Rarely will you be given the opportunity to adapt a work of quality.

The most positive aspect of writing adaptations is that it allows you to polish your craft.

The negative aspect is that it tells you little about the state of your soul.

My advice is to write where the air is clean.

But if you can't—and sometimes you can't—write not only with the heat of your mind, but also with a gas mask.

For the war is far from over.

I have often taken assignments not only because I enjoyed working with the source material, but also because that material seemed to be an organizational (and, therefore, dramaturgical) nightmare.

In other words, a wonderful dramatic problem to be solved.

Several years ago I was asked to adapt Tom Robbins's *Even Cowgirls Get the Blues*.

I had not read the work.

After thirty pages I made the first of three tactical errors:

I accepted.

After all, the book was a delight, and its heroines a pleasure to live with.

What were the errors?

First, there were six producers attached to the project:

Second, there was Tom Robbins's right to approve the final script—a clause no studio ever has granted any writer, and correctly. In effect, it turned the author of the book not only into a seventh producer, but, more, into an unofficial studio head. (Still . . .)

The third error was not to consider the realities of the first two errors: the script had to be voted upon by the six producers and Tom. Thus the politics of realizing the script should have been my major consideration before I accepted to do the adaptation.

I did not think about politics. I thought about the characters.

And yet because I know *Cowgirls* to be the best adaptation I've yet written, and the steps in the adaptation interesting ones, I would like to use the process itself as an example of a method of adaptation:

1) After reading the novel several times, I broke the book down into chapters, with a brief synopsis of each chapter. I would use this for future scene character reference;
2) I cross-referenced the work with character relationships, defining them through chapter and page;
3) I made a breakdown of all the settings.

In this fashion I had the narrative line, character appearances and various settings arranged easily and neatly.

4) I prepared a scene-by-scene outline of the film —as I would like to see it. This allowed me to distance myself from the literary narration and to move towards its cinematic equivalent. I discussed the outline over several weeks with the producers.

Once we were in agreement, I returned to Rome (where I live) to begin the first draft.

Since the novel jumps about in time and space, the film outline would serve to ground me in the movie's own compact narrative reality. The novel breakdown would give me events and character turns, as well as dialogue that could be utilized.

But the film outline was the essential aspect of the material.

As I had mentioned in the section on *Slaughterhouse Five*, the work cannot simply be a random collection of scenes, presented without rhythm and dramatic momentum. Needless to say, the film outline did not structurally follow the novel, although both ended in the same place, and with the same characters, themes, and tone.

I began to write the screenplay.

The cast of *Even Cowgirls Get the Blues* is enormous: the heroine, Sissy Hankshaw; her Thumbs; the Cowgirls themselves; Sissy's husband, and the Countess, and the New York entourage; Sissy's past in Richmond, Virginia.

The first ten minutes of the film would have to introduce practically everybody, set the tone, and create the zany universe of the book.

In the novel, the cowgirls are not introduced until page 90. Sissy's relationship to them does not begin until after page 100. Moreover, much of the earlier part of the novel deals with Sissy's childhood, and her outsized thumbs. Also it is concerned with how Sissy herself had taken up hitchhiking as a way of life.

How to compress one hundred pages of characters, ideas, and very few events into the first ten minutes of screentime?

Even Cowgirls Get The Blues

FADE IN:

1. DAKOTA PLAINS—DAWN

MAIN TITLE BEGINS OVER an electrically-charged violet sky, the faint trace of a pink June sun at its edge: Dawn, on the primordial plain of the Dakotas.

SLOW PANORAMA of this flat, lush, and awesome scape, the sun now starting its rise, to burnish the heavens, fading violet to blue. Asters bend in the dawn breeze, and willowy grass of the prairies. Angels and Elementals are at work in this magical place—sylphs, salamanders, ondines, and gnomes. The landscape glitters. The landscape hums.

CAMERA CONTINUES ACROSS the fields, ending on an outhouse: odd, isolated, seemingly the only sign of mankind on this otherwise timeless part of the planet. CAMERA BEGINS TO TRUCK slowly around the building, finishing at its front. For a moment all is still. Then, surprisingly, the door is kicked open from the inside by what appears to be a demure pair of boots, jeans cuddled coyly around its wings. The door, now open to the dawn, reveals a fabulous photo of Dale Evans, tacked to its inside. The sun rises. *Dale blazes.* It is going to be a fine day.

The boots retire into the outhouse. After a brief moment, its occupant appears: the cutest cowgirl in

the West. Peak-nosed, bright-eyed, nineteen-year-old
BONANZA JELLYBEAN. She takes a deep breath,
looks about happily, and adjusts her milkwhite holster.

She starts to move toward a bunkhouse set in the
distance below a craggy, time-scarred mountain. As
BONANZA walks, or rather struts, she pulls a pearl-
handled revolver from her holster, and twirls it with
affected nonchalance about her finger. Then she flicks
it expertly around her back and to her other hand as if
it were a baton. Humming to herself, and not missing
a beat, she enters the

2.   BUNKHOUSE   SUNRISE

Hazy early morning light falls sluggishly over a long
low room filled with bunkbeds. In each bed, a sleeping COWGIRL.

BONANZA surveys the scene with pride: this is *her*
doing. The first all-girl ranch in the world!

> **BONANZA**
> Okay, cowgirls, rise'n shine!

No one moves, In a far bed, however, and fluttering,
DEBBY, a dark-haired and slightly strung-out Cowgirl,
shoots up, disentangling herself from the arms of
another Cowgirl, KYM.

> **DEBBY** (*Frightened; guiltily*)
> Jesus Christ, Bo, I had a nightmare, honest.
> I was in San Francisco, and this guy came
> up with a needle—

BONANZA (*Good-naturedly; but with disbelief*)
> Just scramble out'a Kym's bunk, Debby.
> (*Beat*)
> And don't call me Bo; it's Bonanza...
> (*Grumbling*)
> Nightmare, my foot...!

She turns on a radio. From two enormous loudspeakers comes "The Starving Armenians Polka," one of a million polkas aired daily on the only radio station in the area.

A collective groan.

ANGLES OF COVERS being pulled back, revealing a thoroughly heterogeneous collection of faces, bodies, a mixed and blessed bag of sleepy-eyed COWGIRLS, some with shaggy hair, others frizzy or Beatle-banged, all of the girls in various phases of drift from sleep to consciousness.

ANGLES OF FEET, large, small, pedicured, calloused, all sweet, all delicious, all hitting the floor.

END MAIN TITLE

BONANZA picks up a day-glo duty roster hanging from the wall, and begins to march down the aisle like a good-natured drill sergeant.

> **BONANZA**
> Let's get it on, girls, sun's comin' up smooth and steady! Big Red and Peel got to mend the goat fence; Debby's got to weed the garden; Kym, aw c'mon hon, you got grub duty an' you ain't even washed yet . . . !

The COWGIRLS groan, stretch, react. BONANZA laughs, setting the roster on the face of a Cowgirl, and plops down, beginning to strip for a shower.

The enormous, green-eyed, Titian-haired Cowgirl, BIG RED, stretches, removing the roster, rising from the bed. She is mythic in size and psyche.
> Hey, y'ol' Big Red, what's shakin'?

BIG RED
Jus' keep ploppin' on my bed like that,
and my jugs'll curdle.

MARY, a bony, freckle-faced, wide-eyed Jesus freak,
turns hotly to RED.

MARY
You're disgusting!

BIG RED shoots BONANZA a conspiratorial look.

BIG RED (*Loudly*)
Hey, Mary? What's got eight legs, eight arms,
four blackheads and four fat wangers?

BONANZA (*Quietly: seriously interested*)
The *Temptations*?

MARY (*Shuddering*)
Stop it!
MARY disappears into the communal shower. BIG
RED grins.

BIG RED (*To* BONANZA)
I already tole you that?

BONANZA
Yup.

BIG RED
Mus' be gettin' old . . . Come on, l'il podner. . . .

They cross to the

3. COMMUNAL SHOWER   DAY

BIG RED reaches for the knob.

Ever see Sissy Hankshaw work these handles?
At the sound of Sissy's name, BONANZA turns,
surprised.

BIG RED (*Continued*)

Shit, I was laughin' so hard they had to clean around me like I was some sick ol' hog.

She turns on the shower. BONANZA looks away.

Immediately BIG RED senses her isolation.

(*Apologetically*)

Hey, Bonanza . . . ?

BONANZA's eyes are starting to brim with tears.

Come on, now, don't get all gooey . . . We all miss her, too. . . . 'Cept for Delores Del Ruby, wherever she may be. . . .

CAMERA FAVORS BONANZA. Instead of the self-conscious hero/heroine in her own Western, she now resembles a very hurt ten-year-old, fighting back tears. She turns on the handle, looking up. The water pours down . . .

MATCH CUT TO:

4.   NEW JERSEY TURNPIKE   NOON

. . . and the rain seems to answer: foul, gray, whipped by a cold and bitter wind. Beneath the sodden downpour, her face besmudged, strawberry blonde hair soaked and hanging in mousecurls, her fawn-colored jumpsuit soiled and tattered, stands SISSY HANKSHAW, a drenched willow in a rainstorm. Lean, Botticellian, pathetic, her right arm extended outward in a desperate hitch, her magnificent right Thumb a brave ship in the North Atlantic.

An enormous diesel truck hurtles by, splashing rain and muck over her body. With a fatality born of the storm, she moves back, tossing the hair from her eyes, squinting through the rain at TWO POLICE

CARS which have moved before her, the COPS staring at SISSY as if she were a pterodactyl recently transferred from swamp to city.

SISSY (*Quietly*)
Oh my...

1ST COP
What the hell you doing?

SISSY
Hitchin' to the city.

2ND COP (*Furiously*)
Get in here! What's your name?

SISSY
Sissy.

2ND COP
Sissy *what*?

He opens the door without descending from the car.

SISSY
Hankshaw Gitche.

1ST COP
The hell kind of name is that?

SISSY climbs into the car.

SISSY
Virginian. With some Mohawk thrown in.

The car careens out into the storm.

5. INT.   JERSEY PRECINCT HOUSE   DAY

The rain continues relentlessly outside. A large, bored OFFICER is fingerprinting SISSY. ONE OF THE COPS stands beside her.

> OFFICER
> Address?

> SISSY
> Fourteen West Tenth Street, Borough of Manhat—

> OFFICER (*Suddenly*)
> My God, would you look at that thumb!

The OFFICER is trying to set SISSY's wet Thumb into the inker.

The Thumb, however, heroic in size, vibrates offendedly, as any decent citizen in a police station would.

> You got some kinda disease?

> SISSY (*Shaking her head*)
> Hunh-unnh . . .

> OFFICER
> The hell'd you do to it?

> SISSY
> Nothin'. They're just big, that's all.

> OFFICER
> Both of 'em?

SISSY shrugs, uncomfortably.
The 2ND COP appears, holding a computer read-out.

> 2ND COP
> Hey, Jim: they got a Missing Persons out on her.

> 1ST COP
> You notify Central?

> 2ND COP
> They're on their way.

SISSY looks about her, confusedly.

OFFICER
What did she do?

SISSY
I didn't do nothin'.

OFFICER (*Toughly; to* SISSY)
I'm not talking to you.

2ND COP
What do you mean, what did she do? She
disappeared.

SISSY
Like I said—

OFFICER (*Ignoring her*)
What's the charges?

2ND COP
No charges.

SISSY (*Glumly*)
Tell a lie, eat a fly.

OFFICER
Yeah, well Manhattan may not have a charge, but
we do: hitching on the New Jersey Turnpike!

SISSY
Well, see, I started my hitch in North Dakota—

OFFICER (*Snorting; to* COP)
Give Thumbelina over here a little walk to the
slammer. Next time, honey, try the bus.

SISSY turns. Rushing to her is a cherubic dumpling of
a man, tanned by indoor GE suns, well-manicured

and wearing pure J. Press: JULIAN GITCHE—Yale
'62, Graphics Designer, Manhattan lover, husband of
Sissy, former Mohawk Indian—in order of preference.

Behind him flits an extraordinary vision: a half-turned
Dorian Gray. Or a fruity version of a Banana Republic
eminence gris, complete with Moluccan cane. He is
THE COUNTESS. In his late sixties, the COUNT-
ESS gives off the stewed look of an Edwardian keeper
of a select male brothel. He is *Death in Venice* come
to New York and making good, *danke*.

Although JULIAN does most of the talking, he appears to be on the COUNTESS's psychic leash. For
the COUNTESS is his livelihood.

> JULIAN
> Sissy! Oh, my God! Officer, give her a blanket—

SISSY looks from JULIAN to the COUNTESS, taken
aback. The rhythm of the road has been broken for
the City. The readjustment is damned near impossible.

> SISSY
> Hi, Julian. I know I shoulda called. I'm sorry.

> JULIAN
> Sorry?

He looks to the COUNTESS for approval of his
line-reading.

> COUNTESS
> We'll talk about it in the car.
> (*To the* OFFICER)
> May I have the ticket, or whatever it is you folks
> dish out?

The OFFICER looks up, trying to see if mockery's
involved. But the COUNTESS smiles sweetly, pulls a
card and fifty dollars from his crocodile billfold.

6.   INT.   COUNTESS'S LIMOUSINE   DAY

Windshield wipers reveal the streaky George Washington Bridge, and the Manhattan skyline.

JULIAN (*O.C.*)
I can't go *on* this way, Sissy. You've been gone a whole month!

CAMERA REVEALS SISSY seated in the rear of the limo, beside an impassive, denture-clacking COUNTESS. Hunched forward uncomfortably, wriggling around so as to see SISSY better, is JULIAN, alone in the jumpseat.

COUNTESS (*Unflappable*)
Twenty-one days, Julian.

JULIAN (*Nodding; sweating*)
I love you, Sissy, but...

COUNTESS (*Prompting, pleasantly*)
...but what you did...

JULIAN
...Yes, what you did is *unspeakable*! I mean, my God, it's...so...whimsically...*adolescent*!

He looks pleadingly at the COUNTESS.

SISSY
Julian, honey, I'm sorry. I didn't want to cause no aggravation.

JULIAN
No? Then why did you *do* it?

SISSY looks out the window, at Manhattan.

COUNTESS (*Sweetly*)
Sissy: for a moment, forget that you are the

squaw of a tender Mohawk. Look deep down into that sweet Virginia soul of yours and ask: "What do I owe Countess?"

SISSY (*Simply*)
A debt o'gratitude.

COUNTESS (*As if to a child*)
And why?

SISSY
'Cause of all the work you guv me—

COUNTESS (*Suddenly snapping*)
Oh, *fluff*! Don't play Miss Melanie with *me*, Sissy Hankshaw! You owe me *loyalty*! Where were you when those rank, strutting sluts took over my ranch?

JULIAN
Yes, and where—

COUNTESS
Hush up, Julian, this is *my* limo!

JULIAN hushes. SISSY looks at him, frowning. She feels his fear, and pities him.

SISSY
When you was on the ranch, I was on the ranch, too. . . .

COUNTESS
Not with *me* you weren't! You were with that massage parlor fugitive, Bonanza Jellybean! That bluegrass Emma Goldman!

SISSY, startled, looks at JULIAN. What has he learned? JULIAN suddenly finds the floor fascinating.

Now Sissy: either you remove any and all links
with a) those barbecue bitches; b) that "on-the-
Road-Hallelujah-I'm-A-Bum" bullshit for which
you have become notorious, or I will sever all of
your ties with the world of fashion, modeling,
publicity.
(*Beat*)
And what I sever of your husband's is best left
unsaid.

The car stops at a light. A street theater is in progress,
based upon Tarot images: The Magus, The Fool, The
Empress dance before a piper in Hermit's garb. SISSY's
eyes light up.

JULIAN (*Quickly*)
Sissy: you need help.

SISSY (*Surprised*)
Huuuuh?

JULIAN
Therapy. You need therapy.

SISSY
I do?
The car starts up, once again.

JULIAN (*Desperately*)
Our marriage is floundering. . . .

SISSY
Hell, Julian, now you know that ain't true.

JULIAN (*Exasperatedly*)
"Isn't," not "ain't!"

SISSY
Ahh, shit, Julian, I do too love you.

COUNTESS (*Drily*)
'Nuff said! Either you go into therapy, Sissy, and
stop your gypsy ways, or I drop the both of you
right here: and bear in mind, we are nearing
One Hundred Twenty-fifth Street and Amster-
dam. . . .

SISSY now stares at JULIAN. He is serious. She
sighs, shaking her head resignedly, looking like a waif
in the prison blanket.

SISSY (*With a kind of comic defeat*)
Well . . . like the Chink says: if it's sloppy, eat it
over the sink.

The novel speaks of Sissy's extraordinary feats of
hitchhiking. In the film we must construct these feats as
Robbins himself constructed Sissy.

In this scene, Sissy explains to her therapist the
psychic reality of hitching (and we *show* it, and don't *tell*
it):

25. **ROBBINS**
So. You came to New York.

SISSY
Not all that soon. . . . I crossed the continent.
Twice in six days. I logged over one hundred and
twenty-seven hours non-stop. Please don't think
me immodest, Doc, but I'm probably the best
there is. When poor Jack Kerouac heard about
me, he got drunk for a week.

ROBBINS (*Surprised*)
Kerouac?

SISSY
Yup. 'Til I met Julian, he's the only one what
interested me.

> **ROBBINS** (*Impressed*)
>
> Amazing.

> **SISSY**
>
> Yeah. But I guess he sorta become professionally
> jealous, the way *I* was doin' the road.

> **ROBBINS**
>
> *Then* you came to New York?

> **SISSY**
>
> Hell, no. I decided I oughta set records 'n see if
> I could break 'em. . . .

VICTOR (the WAITER) appears, setting the hash
before them. SISSY immediately sets about happily
gobbling it up. ROBBINS just stares at her.

> An' unlike ninety-nine percent of the people you
> see thumbin' it these days, doc, I had *style*.
> (*Beat*)
> In the age of the automobile there have been
> many great drivers, but only one great passenger.

> **ROBBINS** (*A whisper*)
>
> You. . . .

> **SISSY** (*Seriously*)
>
> Right on, doc! When I am movin', stoppin' car
> after car, workin' so free 'n so fine 'n so groovy,
> then I embody the rhythm o' the universe.

CAMERA MOVES IN FOR A TIGHT OF SISSY.

(*Beat*)

> Doctor: I know this sounds awful strange. . .

> **ROBBINS** (*Seriously*)
>
> *No . . .!* Not at all. . .

> **SISSY**
> Then will you believe, when I am standin' by the side o' the road, I am in a state o' grace?

FLAT CUT TO:

26. **THE IMMORTAL SISSY HANKSHAW HITCH**
    TIMELESS

A) **FLAT DESERT HIGHWAY**   **DAWN**

LONG SHOT OF THE SUN, a vast, pulsating PINK EGG, enveloping SISSY in its CENTER: The Giver of the Rays. Her right arm is held out straight and firm, Right Thumb erect, an eternal conductor about to give a cosmic downbeat. Full ranging SYMPHONIC CHORD, almost Teutonic in heroism. For Art is about to be summoned to its heights.

The MUSIC, full and rich, follows SISSY rhythmically, *taking its cue from her hitch decisions*, changing tempo as she does, becoming lyrical when she is, or funky and fast when she so desires.

TIGHT OF SISSY'S EYES, all-perceiving, green and gray-flecked, sweeping across the horizon like the lamps of a lighthouse.

The eternal road, and then flickering beams of the most enormous diesel ever constructed, a fiery and snorting mechanical dragon.

SISSY'S THUMB starts to lower like the cannons of the Potemkin.

The DIESEL belches fire, accepting the challenge.

The THUMB-GUN recoils, for a moment, like a snake.

SISSY'S EYES narrow.

LOW ANGLE of the hurricane-DIESEL, a charging rhino.

SISSY'S EYES go wide, sending out beams of BRAKING ENERGY.

Now! The THUMB-CANNON springs forward.

DIRECT HIT! With a multi-toned sigh, and amid an enormous veil of black smoke and sparking tires, the DIESEL brakes.

SISSY smiles coldly.

B) INDUSTRIAL CITY CLOVER LEAF   NOON

The most ingenious maze ever devised by a highway engineer: a spider web spun by the ACID FREAK BLACK WIDOW, with exits and entrances, curves and vast intersections looping and careening drunkenly before and around a smoking inferno of industrial chimneys and pylons. A White Car stops in the center of the maze.

SISSY emerges. Hitches. Catches a lift.

Appears on a higher level of the maze. Stops. Emerges. Hitches. Rides.

Reappears at the bottom of the maze. Stops. Emerges. Hitches. Rides.

Finds herself on a widened curve. Stops. Emerges. Hitches. Rides.

Puts herself at the top of the curve, less than fifty feet from her first hitch. (Stops. Emerges. Hitches. Rides.)

ZOOMS around to the other side. (Stops. Emerges. Hitches. Rides.)

Faster and frequently she stops, loops and curves in the hitch of a ride.

Rides and hitches, scoobydoo, loops and stops and curves and starts, swing that chassis, Gen'ral Mo!

'Til, in a Lamborghini Sprite, she sweeps around the entire maze and disappears in a blaze of Light!

C) NEW ENGLAND ROAD   LATE AFTERNOON

A road through a forest of birches and elms, with evenly-spaced undulations, a lakelike highway constructed in waltz-time.

SISSY floats through like Naughty Marietta in a series of convertibles she herself has especially chosen for the hitch, alternating colors of blue (she's wearing a green jumpsuit); green (in her blue jumpsuit); orange (she's wearing a beige jumpsuit); beige (in her orange jumpsuit).

The final hitch travels down toward a lake, continuing with SISSY in a speedboat, undulating still *in time to* the highway, hitching a larger speedboat and

returning in the original direction, arm out still, THUMB up, to contain a glass of champagne which is placed in her hand.

D) MOJAVE DESERT   LATE AFTERNOON

Sand dunes shimmering in waves of heat. SISSY at the base of a dune, sweating beside her Thumbs, waiting. Then one Thumb grows suddenly erect.

SISSY looks to the top of the dune, wonderingly. Raises her hand, questioningly.

SIX DUNE BUGGIES leap over the top.

And TWENTY-FOUR JETS ZOOM above them, dipping their wings in greeting.

E) HOLLYWOOD BLVD.   EARLY EVENING

SISSY hopscotches over the Stars of Gable and Lombard. Then hitches half a block. Stops.

Dances over the Joans, Bennett and Crawford. Stops. Hitches half a block.

Leapfrogs over W. C. Fields and Orson Welles. Stops. Hitches half a block.

Pauses before the Grauman's Chinese, then leaps in slow motion hard and long and very far to land in the feet of... Marilyn Monroe! Suddenly the Grauman's lights blaze on, all at once, as if in applause.

F) KEYS BRIDGES, FLORIDA   NIGHT

Hurricane winds and rain sweep across the bridges. SISSY, lashed by a belt to one of the bridge rails, leaps out like the Figurehead of the Flying Dutchman and into the storm, snagging a white Rolls. With a foot linked around the bar of the railing, she tosses her belt into the car, the rain and wind tugging at her, threatening to blow her into the sea; great waves reach up for her, but she pulls herself through the tempest, inch by inch, struggling toward the car; for a moment her hands start to slip, and it seems all is lost! But with demonic energy, and a shake of her mane, she moves forward again, her Thumbs grappling with the line. . . . Until a pair of strong arms pull her inside. Safe at last!

G) CHICAGO STREET   DAY

A menacing Black Cadillac pulls up beside a Mercedes, at the intersection of a street. Windows roll down. A machine-gun flares. The Mercedes veers into a lamp-pole. Quickly, from the other side of the Mercedes, SISSY emerges, walking away with embarrassment.

H) LOG JAM ON AN OREGON RIVER   NOON

SISSY sticks out her Thumb, and the entire jam moves toward her.

I) TEXAS GULF   SUNSET

SISSY alone, on a shoal. Her THUMB raises, and a school of porpoises appears. SISSY climbs on the leader's back, and heads to sea.

J) ROAD   EVENING

Headlights in SISSY's wide, unblinking eyes. Headlights dissolving to twin desert moons.

SISSY slowly raises her arm to the Heavens.

The Moons group together as *one enormous crescent*, and descend.

SISSY climbs within the crescent, Left Thumb linked about its bony sweep, right arm and Thumb extended in nocturnal hitch.

The Crescent rising and, within it, SISSY.

Sweeping beyond the sleeping, curving face of America.

And fading, then, among the stars.

FADE OUT.

When Sissy first encounters the cowgirls at the Countess's Rubber Rose Ranch, I was faced with the interesting task of introducing nine specific characters.

Robbins zigs from the introduction in a leisurely fashion. In fact, twenty pages elapse before the cowgirls take over the ranch.

In film, however, this must be accelerated, with none of the loss of vision. I felt that through action the characters could be introduced (Character is Event), and the film moved forward.

44. MOTTBURG MAIN STREET, SOUTH DAKOTA DAWN

A red truck stops and SISSY emerges, looking about her, squinting. The Main Street consists of a crossroads of small stores set in the middle of prairie grass. Infinity. Silence.

SISSY looks around, wearily, begins moving down the main street as a Carry Cadillac comes screeching along, two painted Rubber Roses on its door.

A heavily made-up woman, weighed down with scarves and gold bracelets, leans her head out of the car window. She is Miss ADRIAN.

MISS ADRIAN
Mrs. Gitche?

SISSY
Yes?

MISS ADRIAN
Finally! I'm Miss Adrian, director of the Rubber Rose.

SISSY smiles politely, enters the car.

45. INT. CADILLAC   MORNING

MISS ADRIAN and SISSY are seated in the rear. The COWGIRL BIG RED is driving, all the while eyeing SISSY through the rear-view mirror.

MISS ADRIAN
The photographers are already down at the lake,
setting up for the arrival of those cranes—

BIG RED (*Muttering loudly*)
—Or getting jerked off by six horny cowgirls.

SISSY looks up. BIG RED winks. MISS ADRIAN
tries to ignore her.

MISS ADRIAN
The Countess called this morning—

BIG RED
—Speakin' o' jerk-offs.

MISS ADRIAN (*Stiffly*)
Miss!

BIG RED (*Innocently*)
'Scuse me, Miz Adrian?

MISS ADRIAN (*Sighing*)
Sissy, that is Big Red.
(conspiratorially; nastily)
Her *real* name is Luanne MacDougall . . .

BIG RED
Hi, there . . .

SISSY
Hi . . .

BIG RED
Ain't you the gal does all them cunt ads?

MISS ADRIAN presses a button, and the glass parti-
tion rises between BIG RED and the passengers.

MISS ADRIAN (*Hissing tightly*)
As you can see, I'm having a great deal of troub—

BIG RED slams down the gas pedal, and both MISS ADRIAN and SISSY are thrown backwards; the former becomes bug-eyed; her features seem to be greeting an exceptional exhibitionist.

I hate them I hate them I hate them!

SISSY stares. BIG RED grins at her, in the mirror. Before them, an enormous gate with a sign: WELCOME TO THE RUBBER ROSE RANCH!

46. RANCH   MORNING

The car careens through the gate, pulling up in a cloud of dust before a large, pleasantly trellised ranch-house. SEVERAL WOMEN are doing calisthenics in the main yard.

SISSY and MISS ADRIAN descend. BIG RED sends the Cadillac through the exercisers; they leap, shreiking, out of harm's way.

MISS ADRIAN
Wait 'til the Countess arrives! He'll show those monsters what's what!

They start to move to the ranch-house, but are blocked by a charging "posse" on horseback, consisting of BONANZA, DELORES, GLORIA and MARY.

BONANZA
Miss Adrian, we gotta talk to you!

MISS ADRIAN (*With false sweetness*)
Later, Bonanza! I'm quite busy.

At the name Bonanza, SISSY looks up. The former is dressed in white boots, white mini-skirt, white silk shirt and white Stetson. She resembles the Angel of Milkweed.

BONANZA
I jus' wanna ask yer permission to take care o'
them cows...

MISS ADRIAN (*Stiffly*)
You *are* cowgirls, are you not?

BONANZA shoots the others a conspiratorial look.

BONANZA
Thankee, ma'am, thass all I wanna know, ma'am...

They tear out, with whoops and calls. SISSY watches
them, amazed. MISS ADRIAN takes SISSY by the
arm, leading her to

47. INT. BUNKHOUSE   DAY
A class is seated before make-up tables, learning
about cosmetics, led by PEEL (not yet a Cowgirl).

MISS ADRIAN
As you may know, Mrs. Gitche, we offer the
same program as Elizabeth Arden: diet, mat
exercises, skin care, but at half the price and
twice the fun! What sets us apart, however, is our
program of, well, *intimate* conditioning.

They cross to another room where women are being
shown the various vaginal sprays.

INSTRUCTRESS
Strawberry, if he is tired. *Red Rose Bouquet,* if
he is feeling lusty. *Musk,* to be used *only* in cases
of extreme disfunction. A drop of musk oil on
your fingertips, a gentle whisk across his... better
half, and you'll be amazed by the results!

SISSY (*To* MISS ADRIAN)
Sex education! How do you like that...!

MISS ADRIAN (*Whispering*)
Not quite. How to lure a man to bed and, most important, *once* he's there, how to *keep* him there.

SISSY (*Politely*)
Golly goodness . . .

INSTRUCTRESS
Most men are put off by odors which no longer serve any *real* function. Primitive man lived in a swamp. Nature gave to women the equivalent smell. It is our belief, based upon the most intensive marketing research, that there's no need for the fish market when wildflowers will do.

MISS ADRIAN (*To* SISSY)
The Countess is a genius, Mrs. Gitche. No doubt abou—

A barrage of hideous gunfire. WOMEN SCREAM.

Omigod omigod!

SEVERAL GUESTS rush in from the other room.

1ST GUEST
Miss Adrian!

2ND GUEST
They're killing the cows!

48. PASTURE   DAY

BONANZA and the other COWGIRLS seem to be buffalo-hunting, chasing down the herd with rifles, and shooting. Carcasses of cattle are scattered all over the place. THE CAMERAMEN are filming the slaughter.

SISSY and the horrified MISS ADRIAN rush to the field.

> **MISS ADRIAN**
> Bonanza! What are you doing?

> **BONANZA**
> Puttin' this herd outta its misery, that's what.

> **MISS ADRIAN**
> Stop it at once! Just you wait until I tell the Countess!!

> **BONANZA**
> Yesterday me and the cowgirls seen these long pink worms comin' outa their stools. 'N half them cows got green snot dripping from—

> **MISS ADRIAN** (*Shuddering*)
> That's disgusting! Go back to the bunkhouse!

> **BONANZA**
> You said I's to take care of them cows! What're you running, a ranch or a fairy farm?

> **MISS ADRIAN**
> Into your *room*! Nasty girl!

> **DELORES** (*Exploding*)
> Joo leesen to me, monnkey fess!

MISS ADRIAN turns angrily to DELORES. The latter draws her whip back, menacingly.

> **MISS ADRIAN** (*Fearfully*)
> If you can talk *sense*, I'll listen.

> **DELORES**
> Gwe got seek cows jere, theyyall deeseesed. . . . Gwe try to mek then strawn an' helty, bot joo

geev oss no more monnies. . . . Now theyyall
eenfested an' whan joo haf joor barbakoo, joo
gonna geef evairwan *gwermps!*

MISS ADRIAN (*Uncomprehendingly*)
Gwermps?

BONANZA
Worms, damn your eyes! Before *we* come along,
half them fat ol' bitches got the clap from the
cowpokes! Soon as we kicked 'em out, ev'r'one
got better.

BIG RED (*To* BONANZA)
'Cept fer poor ol' Minnie Lou Morris; got her
tongue caught where angels fear to tread.

BONANZA
'N now she speaks in strange signs 'n foul
gestures. . . .

BIG RED
God rest her soul, ol' Minnie Lou.
(*She crosses herself*)

DEBBY (*To herself*)
My God, Big Red's *Cath*olic!

MARY (*Flouncing*)
Anyway, Billy West has promised to get us a herd
of goats.

MISS ADRIAN (*Shocked*)
Goats?

DELORES
Jess. Gotes. G-o-t-e-s.
(*Muttering*)
Stoopeed cleet!

KYM (*Sweetly*)

Goats are just like *gurus*, Miss Adrian. They can tell when you're faking your feelings, so they constantly test-test-test...

MARY

And they're much cuter than cows.

MISS ADRIAN

We'll see about this! Goats, indeed!

DEBBY

The goat is the most far-out creature on this planet, next to Krishnamurti....
(*To KYM*)
I heard him in Ojai once, when I was with the Manson family? He was so heavy, man, I was high for weeks....

KYM

Oohwow...

DEBBY

"You'll never get into me," he said, "until you're out of yourself."

KYM

Heavy...

BONANZA

Anyways, though I'd rather be a cowgirl than a goatgirl, Miss Adrian, we got ourselves a herd comin' in, and that's just tough luck fer the cows.

MISS ADRIAN (*Suddenly snapping*)
Miss Jellybean? You-are-*fired*!

Stunned silence. BONANZA pales.

BONANZA (*A teen-age rage*)
If I leave, you gonzo bitch, I'm takin' these cowgirls with me!

The COWGIRLS mutter words of support.

Hell, I brought 'em here, every one of 'em, *hand*-picked!

MISS ADRIAN
We'll find others, Little Miss!

BONANZA
Podners?

The COWGIRLS look at each other, with hidden meaning. Suddenly BIG RED takes her lassoo, roping MISS ADRIAN.

BIG RED
C'mon, Miss Addie...there's a whole lot o' shakin' goin' on...!

She begins to trot across the field, with MISS ADDIE racing along to keep up. BONANZA turns to SISSY.

BONANZA (*Threateningly*)
What about *you*?

SISSY
Huunh?

BONANZA
You *fer* us or agin us?

SISSY (*Smiling openly*)
I just got here, but I think *you're* neat, really I do....

DELORES (*Snapping*)
Doan leesen to whore! Chee gwan off thaym! I seen hair peechers, all over the fockeen contry! Chee the Countess's sheety seembol!

BONANZA
That true?

SISSY (*Genuinely surprised*)
I ain't the Countess's *anything*...!

BONANZA
What's yer name?

SISSY
Sissy Hankshaw.

BONANZA's jaw drops in surprise. Then she breaks her look.

BONANZA (*Quickly*)
Debby? Go to the shed, get some shears an' cut all them telephone wires! Gloria, get everybody's car keys, put 'em under my bunk 'n hightail it over to Billy West's. Tell 'im to get his butt over here.
(*To SISSY*)
C'mon, podner...

To DELORES's amazement, BONANZA lifts SISSY onto the back of her horse.

SISSY
What we doin'?

BONANZA
Sump'n we shoulda done years ago...! *Revoltin'!*

With a shout, she urges on her horse. The COWGIRLS follow with whoops and yells.

49. SEXUAL RECONDITIONING ROOM   DAY

The WOMEN are gathered around a bidet, staring at it as if it were the Elgin Marbles.

INSTRUCTRESS
The proper way to wash your private parts—

BONANZA enters brusquely, followed by SISSY and the COWGIRLS.

BONANZA
'Scuse me, ev'r'body, but there's been a change in the curriculum.

She nods to DELORES, who throws all the spray cans in the air. BONANZA pulls out her pearl-handled pistol, blasts them apart. The WOMEN cower, terrified. BONANZA nods to KYM.

KYM (*Clearing her throat; to the WOMEN*)
Only a masochist would dip his genitals into benzethonium chloride. And any woman who sprays *hers* with it is a clod.

PEEL appears with the other ladies.

PEEL
Bonanza, what's going on?

BONANZA
Take yer ladies over there, Peel Donnelly. I'm givin' a lesson in self-celebration.

The WOMEN cross to a corner of the room, surprised.

Now you ladies *reely* wanna excite a man 'til he's beggin' fer mercy? Wotcha do is reach down with yer fingers, like this, see, and get 'em all wet with yer juices. Then ya rub it behind yer ears. . . .

The WOMEN resemble multiples of Lot's wife.

Put a dab of it on yer throat an' let it dry. It's the best perfume Ma Nature ever provided, let me tell ya. In Europe, all them high-class Neapolitans like Sophia Loren 'n Ann-Margaret use it. That's why they're so seductive to Heads o' State 'n big guns everywhere . . . Power to the Pussy!

BONANZA looks at SISSY happily and self-righteously
then turns and leaves, followed by the COWGIRLS

The WOMEN remain stunned. They begin to crack
in pieces, like Tom Cat after a successful shot by Jerry
Mouse.

50. EXT. RANCH   DAY

BIG RED drags a dusty and exhausted MISS ADRIAN
toward the ranch-house as BONANZA emerges from
the Conditioning Room.

> **BIG RED**
> What we gonna do now, Bonanza?

> **BONANZA**
> Lock her in the toolshed.

> **MISS ADRIAN**
> No! Please!

> **BONANZA**
> You gonna cooperate with us, or ain'cha?

> **MISS ADRIAN** (*Tearfully*)
> My God, whatever do you want?

> **BONANZA**
> Take all them exercycles 'n beedays 'n shit, put
> 'em in a pile an' burn 'em.
> (*To DELORES*)
> See that she does it, too.

DELORES leads the defeated MISS ADRIAN away.

> (*To the others*)
> Now let's get to buryin' them cows 'fore they
> draw flies . . .

SISSY is transformed, wearing the look of awe and of
wonder she'd evinced during the Richmond parade.
She stares at BONANZA with delight.

As the GIRLS start to move toward the pasture, a heavy whine is heard. All look up.

In the sky, an extraordinary sight: a HELICOPTER is moving above them, with the fattest GOAT on the planet suspended by ropes around its belly! The Response of the Immortal Director Pan to the Mortal Fellini's opening image of *La Dolce Vita*.

Slowly, the monstrous GOAT is lowered. The GIRLS stare in awe. MARY falls to her knees, crossing herself.

MARY
"For He shall reign forever and ever . . ."

DEBBY raises her hands as a Priestess, the tears streaming down her cheeks.

DEBBY
Hare Krishna, Hare Rama, Hare Hare Hare . . .

BIG RED squints up from her horse, chewing gum laconically.

BIG RED (*Almost a whisper*)
*Marl*boro Country . . .

The GOAT descends slowly. TIGHT OF HIS EYES: red hot, goat-wise, horny. He surveys the GIRLS with all the intelligence and lust of the Horned Piper. But, soft! he seems to be thinking: methinks this ranch, 'twill be no sottish spot for a frolic!

FADE OUT.

Now "the charm's wound up," the characters introduced, the conflicts stated through the clash of character.

The rest was simple: as long as the film remained within the same tone, mood; as long as it was consistent with the universe presented in the first ten minutes of film.

Adapting the novel was, for me, a celebration not only of Robbins's work, but also of the potential of film itself.

A rare and challenging opportunity.

Stillborn.

For when the six producers had voted on the script, they decided that I would have to return to Los Angeles to explain each line to them. I refused. If I had to revise the script, I would only do it with Robbins himself—as long as he was involved in the process.

They voted. It was a split vote.

And so the script was never shot.

The moral of this tale: do not fall in love with a wonderful work owned by six producers.

And yet screenwriting *is* an art.

Screenplays can be read as dramatic literature, and certainly should be written with the knowledge that every line or image owes its existence to a rich tradition of theater, painting, and fiction.

Admittedly it has taken the world a long time to realize that a play is not only a tool for actors, but also something more. In spite of clipped stage directions, or shorthand character descriptions, a universe *does* unfold, and in the privacy of the readers' minds. There is *every* reason why the same argument can be made for screenplays. There is *every* reason for you to write hard, to write well, to write deeply, caringly, and with a lust for language.

There is *no reason* why you should consider your work a mere blueprint for other artists or technicians.

But I'll tell you the reasons, anyway.

Part Four:

The Realities of Screenwriting

Some Sobering Thoughts Before We Begin

Motion pictures adapted from another medium generally are the deprived children of that rotten marriage of art and business—which means, most American films. There is no other medium which has relied as heavily upon other artistic associations for its survival. Whereas Western theater has as its origin ritual and the Mysteries, utilizing the collective myth of a culture for its substance, modern American film wallows in the present tense of culture, attempting to create its own myths from instant and popular notions about the world, from popular books, plays, or newspaper headlines.

In modern American films, the muses are not invoked; rather, bets are hedged.

A bestselling novel, record album, or Broadway hit, according to most studio heads, has a built-in audience. Therefore, if the studio is going to spend a great deal of money attracting superstars, it had better show a return. (Although it can be argued that Shakespeare himself used standard sources for his work—notably Plutarch's *Lives* and Holinshed's *Chronicles*—they hardly can be considered the "bestsellers" of their time, the *People* magazine or six o'clock thirty-second "in depth" reportage.)

For these reasons, rarely does a film which has been derived from another medium come into its artistic own; rarely does it leap beyond the boundaries of its original source, and thereby expand the vocabulary of film itself. In American motion pictures I can only think of a few adaptations of the past ten years which give the sense of being born as film: *2001, Hair, Paths of Glory, Lonely Are the Brave, The Stunt-Man*....(I would enjoy adding *One Flew Over the Cuckoo's Nest, The World According to Garp,* even *Slaughterhouse Five* to the list but, however cinematically authentic, those works still very much remain the voice of the original authors—Kesey, Irving, Vonnegut.)

Implied in this argument is my belief that *all screenplays should be originals, written directly for the screen,* and not based upon materials from another medium— unless those materials supply a point of artistic departure. For as long as film remains tied to another source, it will be subjected a hundredfold to the demands of studios and producers; it must remain "faithful" to the source. The film medium therefore will continue to be nothing more than a moving photograph of a playscript, or printed page. It will not have the chance to develop on its own.

John Simon has written that great books do not make great films, but bad books often do.

To a large degree, Simon is correct: bad books or plays often become a creative point-of-departure, a sort of mandala for the writer or director, a jumping-off or leaping-in place, and which nobody sees as an end in itself.

Sadly, most studios or producers can't tell a good book from a bad.

The stock rule-of-thumb is this: if the book is a best-seller, it must be good. So be faithful, scribe. Treat it as writ.

I recall adapting one such novel.

Among many howlers the work contained was the following exhortation from wife to police-husband: "Oh, Francis, Francis, don't you *know* why you're a great detective? Honestly, don't you *know?* Why, you believe in *Beauty!*"

When I argued for excision, the director informed me

that it was an honor to be on the project; more, he said he was an *auteur*...!

Why did I accept the assignment to adapt that novel?

Because the situation of the book, however trashily written, was interesting, and could give us a point-of-departure for an exciting thriller. At the time I did not realize that the director believed the book to be equal to *Crime and Punishment*. (Our working relationship began to resemble that of Raskolnikov and the Landlady, with the director and I occasionally alternating roles.)

Oh dear.

How, then, to write an adaptation without feeling like a handmaiden to the Whore of Babylon?

The following four conditions are necessary to assess before you decide to accept or to reject an adaptation. Give yourself the appropriate number of points for each condition:

1. Is the book a bestseller? An international bestseller? (1 point; 2 points)
2. Does the producer and/or studio and/or director "believe" in the work? (2 points if the work is part of the Entity's belief-system; 3 points if it is to become a shrine)
3. Is your faith in the work as great as the Entity's? (1 point if no; 2 points if yes)
4. Is your faith in yourself greater than your faith in the author of the source material? (1 point if yes; 2 if no)

If you find yourself with five or more points, do NOT accept the assignment; five or less, and you have a chance of making something out of nothing. As flippant as this sounds, these four conditions legitimately will determine the artistic direction of the screenplay, and your working relationship with the studio.

Why?

Because five or more points means that you will end

up being the faithful scribe, with little chance to write. You may also be replaced by another writer after the first draft, for the director will realize that *something is wrong* . . . the book wasn't wrong, so it must be you.

Five or fewer points gives you the chance to write a movie which might stand on its own, *owing very little to another medium*.

If this sounds harsh and unfair to novelists—to say nothing of producers and directors—let it be said that novelists receive money for their work. Money buys time to write more novels. If you are a novelist, you will think greatly about such matters when a producer tells you that your book would make a fabulous film, and offers you a year's grace in the form of an option-against-purchase price.

If you are independently wealthy, you may tell him to do unto himself what he is about to do unto an audience.

If not, thank him for the excellence of his judgment, and take his money.

The principal responsibility of the screenwriter is to the screen.

Although the basic work has originated in another medium, it still must be translated into film language—which is not the same as that of the novel. The screenwriter should possess the novelist's larger vision, a working knowledge of the thematic thrust of the book; yet, at the same time, he must operate within the immediacy of the dramatists' craft, *the present tense of the stage itself*.

This is one of the reasons why there are few decent film adaptations. Either the film version is so respectful of the novel that it sacrifices the immediacy of the moment, or it does not realize how the characters are imbedded in the themes, and so attempts to create new characters, or to manipulate the old ones in a contradictory fashion.

As of this writing, for every twenty-six screenplays written for studios and/or producers (hired pens—not pens which write of their own), *only one screenplay actually is filmed*. In other words, the odds are 26-to-1 that you actually will see your work produced. To compound the nastiness, the economic situation will get worse before it gets better. Ironically, it is possible to develop a fine reputation as a screenwriter *without one page of your work ever being filmed*. The milieu is small. Your abilities are touted. Your price increases.

And most likely you will be living well, if not beyond your means, as the years pass. You will bind your unseen pages in Moroccan leather, and they will preen on your shelves for nobody but you. After ten years you will begin to wonder if *television* is the answer. You certainly will have lost the discipline to write a novel, for the money isn't as good, the lunches and gossip aren't as juicy, and it is so much easier to con a producer out of cash than it is an editor—if only because the editor has a smaller budget, lives in New York, and is too miserable to be susceptible to your charm.

For everyone in film has charm.

It is part of the craft.

After ten years of writing, you will have learned to knot your jowls like Redford (macho thought), to grin like Richard Dreyfus (street-smart coy), and to flash a smile just like Newman (boyish, is spite of all).

I am not being sexist.

The jowl-rent, eye-wink, and smile-flash belong to us all.

More, you may develop eccentricities of such skill that you will be photographed beside Joan Didion, or other Ishmaels who have lived to tell the tale—in the pages of *People*, or other cultural digests.

Charm and Moroccan leather.

And, of course, the gut fear that one day the bubble will burst or—worse!—a script of yours *actually will be filmed*.

What if this occurs?

What if the Goddess of Mirth decides that your day has come?

Then other "elements" will enter the scene: hydrocarbons and gases, stars, and a director.

All will have ideas.

And all will possess charm.
A deadly combination.

The director of photography might well be a superstar. When the script calls for a TIGHT OF MONIQUE's
LEFT EYE, he will set the camera in a helicopter above
Niagara Falls. The director, whom everyone has called
"the writer's best friend," will be outraged, for *he* has
insisted the camera be set in the jungles of Borneo.

But eventually intelligence will triumph.

The actress playing Monique will not understand her
motivation, your scene will be thrown out, another one
quickly improvised at her agent's, then shot in a dentist's
office in Glendale.

There will be battles lost and won, scribe, for fair
indeed can be made foul and, sometimes, foul made to
appear fair.

The Goddess of Mirth, however, presents you with
many options:

1. Fight the rascals, and be kicked off the set. (In all
   likelihood you won't be allowed near it, anyway.)
2. Take the money and invest it in thoroughbreds.
   (The race is less dicey.)
3. Remove your name from the screen (and risk
   losing a percentage of the tv sale).
4. Use your charm, call them all geniuses, then write
   a savagely satirical article for *Esquire* or *Playboy*.
   (The readers won't know your true reputation,
   anyway, and will consider you a bright twenty-five-
   year-old, sensitive to poesy and stunned by the
   oh-so-silly *mores* of that oh-so-silly town—which
   has kept you in very expensive weekends at very
   dull places, but that's not part of the article.)

A list of expensive screenwriters with no credits at all,
or very expensive screenwriters with the most embarrassing
credits in film history will be supplied upon request.

Chto dyelat, as a wise Slav once asked: *What is to be
done?*

Short of nuking of the place and starting over (or letting the Great Mother take her course, and watching the Pacific Coast burp its way towards Japan), there are a variety of ways to survive the barrage of witless, mindless, greedy, egomaniacal, spineless, misanthropic, plotting, soulless, humorless shitheels against (and in spite of) whom one finds oneself constantly UP.

But before I give you the answers, let us examine the problem step-by-step, starting from the top (where the money is), and working our way towards the bottom (where the money sometimes reaches).

1. The Studios

They used to be dirty great places where nearly one hundred films were dreamed per year, and practically per studio.

Now they mainly serve to distribute films.

Last year only seventy-eight films were made in the United States, and a little over half by the studios themselves.

Most of the studios are in crisis, or have been purchased by multinationals, or have become great real-estate investments. One studio, in fact, has been purchased by a former shopping-mall mogul who is divesting the place of its former glory. Where stars once walked, condos rise.

The studios still make films, yes. But at a very big price—not only for the banks, but for the audience as well.

Why?

Because by and large the studio heads are lawyers, former agents, marketing researchers. This means that *the ledger decides*, and not the passions of heart, mind, and soul. This means that much "product" (note the word) is conceived in an accountantlike atmosphere, where the elements of past performance are added together, and the highest sum survives.

The alchemy, the magic of combinations, the very *uncertainty* that has produced outstanding work is no longer part of the equation.

Small wonder that cocaine-cum-*est* is a burgeoning side-product.

How does this actually work, this art-and-accountancy?
Or, to use the industry phrase, this "Packaging"?
You are a studio head.
I am a pleader of film causes.
I say to you: I can offer you a thriller. It stars Jane
Fonda. It will be directed by Alan Pakula. Remember
Klute? Oh yes, it will cost a fortune but it will net you an
even greater fortune! If you don't like it, I can offer you a
teeny-tiny film about four kids growing up in the Midwest,
who ride bicycles and dream of the big race. It'll cost less
than Fonda's hairdresser.

Wily studio chief that you are, you examine the
"elements," the noxious fumes of my proposal. And you
choose *Rollover* over *Breaking Away*.

Wrong.

For that decision you will be fired and asked to
become the head of another studio.

Where, once again, we will meet.
And I will offer you Al Pacino (hot off *Godfather II*),
and directed by Sidney Pollack (hot off *The Way We Were*).
Or would you rather a smallish film about—stop right
there?
And so *Bobby Deerfield* is born . . . !
Very few stars are better than the script.
A good director is only as good as the text, though a
very fine director is often better.
Contrary to most studio thinking, a film that costs a
fortune will not necessarily make a fortune.
As long as studio chiefs refuse the more passionate
functions of the (optimist that I am) mind, leaving themselves victims of somebody else's accountancy as well as
their own laziness, such mocking decisions will continue to
be made until the studios go broke (which they often do).
The typical excuses: "The unions are breaking our
backs," "TV has murdered us," "Kids only go to videogames,"
are projections of the death wish, a means of marking time
until retirement and/or bust.
Strangely enough, many of the younger studio executives not only share this accountant's mentality, but also

actively rationalize their lack of passion *by rejecting everything that comes their way*—in the hope that Jane Fonda or Al Pacino will drop into their offices, followed by Alan Pakula and Sidney Pollack—"oh, and what was the script?"

A list of these executives to be avoided will be supplied upon request.

Still, let us assume the little tads are merely making their way, testing the waters. By the time they're forty, will they appear like Henry IV behind the "base, contagion" smog, and kick the rascals out?

Not bloody likely.

For charm and fear has cleaned their own houses of courage and taste. The rest is just gummy, and oozes out of their ears.

What is to be done?

Still your heart.

There's more yet to be analyzed.

2. The Independents

With the film-making function of the studios grown crabby, if not senile, a new race of man has been delivered unto us: the indie-prod, or independent producer.

He it is who attempts to sell a "package" to a studio: script, cast, star, budget.

He it is who functions as the studios' "minister-without-portfolio."

He may be a very good man or woman.

She may be a very good man as well.

But the indie-prod walks a fine line between accountancy and art.

Let it be said that in sixteen years of busy business, I have yet to work with *one* indie-prod who actually accomplished what he set out to do: to make a fine film.

The indie-prod will often sound like one of us.

He will articulate the visual in thematic terms, or the thematic in visual, or something like that. In any event it will sound very nice.

It will be the job of the studio executive to find the indie's weak spot and to exploit it.

When this happens, the indie-prod will become frightened, and so will cease to sound like you and me.

More often than not he will end up being more "Studio" than the Studio itself. If he is not eventually absorbed by the system, he will learn to grow soybeans. Or marry Japanese.

With one indie-prod less, the studio execs will have one less decision to make. Which seems very much to be their function, anyway.

Life is quite difficult for the indie-prod.

3. The Directors

They used to be handed scripts by the studios, and told to shoot or be shot.

They came from theater, and knew that in order to tell the story they had better understand character.

They made films on time, and within the budget.

Constantly under the gun of unemployment, they had little time to reflect on film as art.

Consequently, art emerged.

Then came the *nouvelle vague* and, with it, the vague news that directors were actually *auteurs;* without a doubt, if the director wrote his own work, or at the very least collaborated with a writer, then the dread appellation made sense. But, *hélas*, no. Every director, according to a misreading of those self-advertisements of Godard *et Cie*, (and what have many directors become, but misreaders?), soon was bound for glory.

Many American film critics, invisible men when the lights are on, rushed to proclaim the latest French *bon mot*.

And, since the studio no longer exercised the hire-fire power of the past, the director emerged as superstar. A potent force indeed.

In order to create a "package" pleasing to the economic palate of the accountant-chief, the indie-prod had to woo the *auteur*, promising him everything in order that he himself might walk boldly into the main office to make his pitch.

Suddenly the director-for-hire had another bargaining point: the simple fact that he was called . . . gosh . . . "director?"

Now the writer not only had/has the indie-prod and

studio to deal with, but also the lynch-pin of the wooden package: *l'auteur.*

A tee shirt complains: "Yes, but I'd rather be a director."

It has come to that.

The screenwriter generally can trust a director who has emerged from theater. (Not Polish theater, or off-off Awful).

The screenwriter *sometimes* can trust a director who has "grown up" in television. (This year's studios—but grown up *how,* or *how* grown-up?)

The screenwriter *is in trouble* with a director who shoots commercials, or who has moved directly from film school to studio, with no life somewhere in between. ("After all, if Jerry Brown can do it in politics, why can't I do it in film?")

Why is the screenwriter in trouble?

Because the latter kind of director has ideas, improvements, another way of telling the same and, therefore, *different,* story.

The latter type of director, as he himself so often says, "thinks in visual terms"—which means he does not think in *story terms* at all. Mainly because he never has had to tell a story at all.

Since it is your duty to explain to him exactly why you wrote what you wrote the way you wrote it, you will end up offending him, no matter how soothing your words or charming your manner.

Remember: the indie-prod needs you to write a script in order to have something to sell. (The boy-wonder, Irving Thalberg, called writers "a necessary evil." Charming fellow.) The indie-prod is at your mercy until you have written the script. Then the roles swiftly are reversed.

And also remember: the indie-prod needs to hire a director to make the package tasty to the accountant. Both you and the indie-prod are therefore at the director's mercy until he says yes. You will find yourself rewriting the screenplay according to the director's desires (and so will half a dozen other screenwriters, whose indie-prods are *also* wooing *the same director* for his servicing, and at the same time), until that magical moment when the Big D deigns to acknowledge your efforts.

Then other problems will begin.

Other voices, other tombs.

4. The Agents

After the above barrage, this may surprise you:

I like agents.

They are the legitimate voice of the industry.

They can be overwhelmingly helpful in securing a performer or pursuing the right producer.

The good agents listen. They play angles. They calculate, even as you speak. If they are genuinely creative (in other words, if they enter in to the subject of your script and toy with casting possibilities), they are invaluable.

Most agents know how to read.

Contrary to complaints, they *do* earn their ten percent.

An agent's role is to keep you informed of the marketplace, and to keep you in it. And once you are in it, to negotiate the main points of your contract: your fee, broken down into steps: first draft payment, first draft revised, percentage points of *the mythic producer's profits*, your *per diem* if traveling is involved, etc.

An agent has to understand your own demands, ego, vainglory, sensitivity, and to deal with it elegantly. Some agents play games. They must. Everyone else does. But if agents satisfy the writer, director, producer, and studio, then they in their own way have performed the greatest hat-trick of all: they have taken warring elements and made of them a blend that will become a film.

Unfortunately, some agents must also represent big performers.

And their performances therefore must mirror the demands of their clients. If this is a clue to the indie-prod of the shape of things to come, he/she should immediately leave the agent's office and seek help elsewhere. For no good will come of it. Nobody is worth that much.

(A list of such agents, as well as good agents, will be supplied upon request.)

Fortunately, few directors or performers are that big. So few agents behave in such a manner.

As clinical psychologists who work in the violent wards of mental institutions possess a macabre sense of humor to stay well, so, too, do agents.

That, more than any other reason, is why I like them.

5. *The Performers*

Once, when I was complaining of a performer's *welshing* on a contract in a film I was to direct, my agent said, "Don't forget: it was an *actor* who shot Lincoln."

There are creative performers, and there are *artists*. The latter type often tell an interviewer, or anyone who is willing to listen, "Basically I like to get this rapport going with the director; then, you know, like I improvise my scenes from this inward need."

No-no.

The writer did not spill blood for a year so that the performer could bear his soul *en rapport*. Every six months such artists should be made to play theater from the back of a van.

There are, however, *stars*.

Cary Grant is a star. Monroe was a star, and James Dean. Magic occurs as soon as their faces are imprinted on celluloid. It doesn't even matter what they do. Or what you have written.

But our Lady of Celluloid kisses few brows.

Most performers must sweat the big drop.

Many times they can be helpful to the writer—if they are able to see beyond their role. But that is not why they are being hired. So why bother? Unless, like most people in the industry, you are star struck.

Then you are in trouble.

In England they order these matters better.

Thespians trod the boards at an early age, playing every sort of role in every sort of theater. By the time they're twenty-five, they have traveled the geography of place and person, have slummed about sufficiently to be happy to earn a decent wage. And keep still.

Sorry.

Writers should write.

Directors direct what is written.

Actors perform the pages they have been handed.

But in Hollow-land it usually doesn't work that way.

6. The Writers

Part of the problem.

Many screenwriters, faced with the pressures implied in this amalgam of egos and notions, simply fold their tents after one huge argument with director, indie-prod, or artist. Why bother doing battle? they think. You can't win, anyway. Take the money, run to complain to your friends in Malibu. . . .

There is no one in the film industry more boring or sillier than the screenwriter spurned.

Ten screenwriters in a room inevitably will begin to complain, to inveigh against the injustices heaped upon them. But none will say what they have done to fight this injustice.

The Writers' Guild certainly protects their salaries and credits.

But, unlike the Dramatists' Guild, it *never* has made an effort to protect their scripts. And screenwriters make up the Writers' Guild. It is, after all, our union, presided over by elected officials.

There is no question that an adaptation is subject to heavy traffic.

But an original screenplay should remain the vision of its author—not its director or *artiste*. (Even as I write this, a good friend and fine screenwriter has called me, complaining that he has been kicked off his own original screenplay. The indie-prod, whom he had considered a friend—*ha!*—had cowered before the political claims of two studio in-fighters.) With stories of such brazen villainy, it is no wonder the screenwriter nags, or dries up, or becomes bitter.

This does not mean, however, that the situation is without a solution. This does not mean that the battle is over before it has begun. Being a lover of film, I prefer the cavalry over Calvary.

Help, therefore, is on its way.

Towards a Solution

1. Movies

In the famous press conference scene of *8½*, a female English journalist turns to the camera and exults: "He has nothing to say! The director has nothing to say!"

To which the producer doubtlessly would reply, "He's not being paid to *say anything*, lady, but to entertain. If you want a message, go call your answering service."

Both points-of-view are at the heart of the tension within the screenwriter: how far should he allow himself to pursue his own private visions? Should he take the liberty of deciding that his vision is not "entertainment," and therefore not worth pursuing? Or should he pursue his vision at the cost of "entertainment?"

What is entertainment?

In its most basic form, entertainment is what people pay money to see.

Mister Producer may not have bothered to see *8½*, but others did. Fellini may not have cared a fig about Mister P's *Cokehead Killers at American High*, but cokeheads, killers, and demented high school students kept said producer alive and well in his studio, where he presently is preparing *Cokehead 2*.

Although I do not share the French critics' enthusiasm for Mister P's abysmal *oeuvre*, I cannot deny his commercial reality any more than ever I would deny Fellini's artistry (*as well as* his commercial reality).

This is a big planet, and there is room for works equal to 8½, or as moronic as P's. Most of us grind our way somewhere in between.

My advice is simple: *Don't worry about the debate between commerce and art*. The public generally decides, by word and by pocketbook, what your work merits.

Any director who tells you what will "play" has a limited view of human possibilities.

Any producer who tells you what the public wants is committing a solitary act in public.

Any critic who tells you what is art is, well, a critic.

Write what excites you, thrills you, keeps you waiting for the next day so that you may write again.

If you create characters from the force of your excitement, your characters themselves will create an audience.

Often I have been criticized for this ostensibly vain and/or egocentric and/or purist attitude. I do not consider it vain or purist at all. Rather, I believe is has to do with staying alive and sane and interested in the possibilities of writing. It has to do with following my characters where they will take me, at the expense of the generalizations of critics and producers alike.

At the expense of ghosts.

To determine what is commercial or artistic *before a line is written, a scene filmed, a novel published*, is time-wasting and nonproductive.

As if this were not obvious, let me cite another great schism in the minds of many critics and Mister P:

What is artistic is not commercial.

Therefore, what is commercial is not artistic.

Chaplin, Keaton, Bergman, Fellini, Allen, Weir, von Trotta—to name only a few—have given the lie to the great schism. Works of art—*Modern Times, The General, The Seventh Seal, La Dolce Vita, Manhattan, The Last Wave, Marianne and Juliane*—also can be commercial hits.

The point of this diatribe is a simple one:

Write from your deepest enthusiasms, nightmares, obsessions, interests, pulse.

Concern yourself with the *force* of your characters. They themselves, in the toss-and-turn of their lives, will create the idea of your piece.

Their tumbling will create an audience.

2. You

Where there's life, there's hope—thought Anna Karenina, as she stepped onto the tracks.

A screenwriter never need assume any working situation to be either-or.

As long as the writer feels, thinks, intuits, when faced with Mr. P's family he is presented with a minimum of three options:

1. Fight.
2. Surrender.
3. Retreat, and gather strength, marking time until deciding the next move.

The pressures that any writer feels often are of his own making, and spring from his own anxieties or ghosts.

The work situation *can be placid*.

After all, you are being paid for your expertise.

Have faith in the more-than-distinct possibility that you can solve the writing problem before you.

Listen *graciously* to suggestions, but accept nothing until you have had a chance to analyze the dramatic realities of those suggestions. Then, *and only then*, decide whether you wish to make them.

It is nice to be patted on the head for your efforts.

Four months of work, after all, of dreaming and struggling through the first draft, deserves a pat. It takes a certain strength to make the pen leap, and even greater strength to keep it leaping. Therefore, do not burst into tears at the first critical thrust into your domain.

However, more often than not the production situation is politically unstable. The studio's producer, the indie-prod, the director, all are jockeying for positions of control.

Still, there *is* room for compromise.

Certainly there are producers, directors, and an occasional star who possess a highly skilled theatrical sensibility, and who can improve the original material.

Why, then, are there so few fine films?

Because more often than not what appears to be artistic improvement is actually political compromise.

Writing is not and never has been a group activity.

At the very least, it is a craft. At the very best, an art. What, said the sage, is a camel?

A greyhound, designed by a committee.

Know that if you enter the political fray, you most likely will be eaten alive.

In any event, you've already done *your* battle, which is to write a screenplay.

Therefore your only loyalty should be to the script itself.

If the changes suggested or demanded move the work into another territory, bear in mind that you will be on the job for at least another six to eight months. The work inevitably will move from A1 to A3 to A7 to A19—and then will finish at L15.

Had you been hired to write L15 in the first place, would you have accepted the assignment?

It is better for you to walk off the project, claiming artistic differences. This is a legitimate reason, and announces that you stand by your work, violently disagree with the direction it has taken, and probably have a good chance in the long run of being proven right—a minor consolation, considering the amount of work you've done. (The technique of the "walk-off" will be explained shortly.)

Therefore, the first part of the solution to the problem facing every writer in the film world—*the politics of that world*—is to possess a legitimate sense of your own worth.

You have spent many years learning your craft, practicing it, sometimes even indulging in foreplay with a mischievous Muse.

Nobody owes you anything, after all; but you owe yourself a great deal.

Do not forget this.

An Example

Let us assume you have turned in your first draft.

The indie-prod is thrilled. It's exactly what he wanted. (His words.)

The director is, well, interested and, of course, has ideas:

Your heroine, Alceste, for example. . . . She shouldn't be French. Rather, a Thai transvestite prostitute. Admittedly this might give the narration a different thrust, *"but-it-just-might-work."*

The indie-prod is terrified, but says nothing. You are, after all, the writer. This is your fight.

What do you do?

First: you tell the director that his ideas are certainly interesting. Secretly, you review the three rules of battle: fight, surrender or retreat.

You decide to fight.

You explain why you feel Alceste would be better as a French girl. You would, for example, have a difficult time writing the scene where Larry introduces Alceste to his mother. Unless, of course, the director wants a comedy? Oh no no no! you are assured. But the director still feels *"the-change-just-might-work."*

You back away from the fight, making a feint in the direction of surrender (while actually retreating).

Very well, you say. But you will need another six months to completely rewrite the screenplay. You will *also* need to go to Bangkok to interview Thai transvestite prostitutes. (Unless this happens to be the director's secret "thing"—i.e., he is living with one.) Once you do take a month to conduct the interviews, then spend another six months rewriting, will the director, sir, still be around to read the completed work? Or will he have started one of the fifteen other films he is preparing?

But even more important, will the indie-prod please call your agent? After all, since this is to be a completely new screenplay, newer financial terms must be discussed. You yourself are uncertain of the new direction of the script, but if the indie-prod genuinely thinks it's worth exploring, then you will—as America's splendid *auteur*, Sylvester "Sly" Stallone has grunted elsewhere—"go the distance."

This pleasant pseudo-surrender has accomplished two ends: it has thrown the battle back into the lap of the indie-prod, where it genuinely belongs. He must now consider the changes himself. He must also evaluate the emotional stability of the director.

Naturally the prod will reply that he sees no difference in the story—just a geographical and sex change. (He is marking time as well.)

You then ask him with whom he would rather sleep: with Alceste, or with the mysterious Pho Ngk? No, you are not being difficult. You merely need a trip to Bangkok and a new contract. And, by God, in another six months you'll certainly come up with the goodies!

You have fought.

And fought again, while seeming to surrender. Never have you lost your core, your artistic center. You took the assignment because you adored Alceste, and not the mysterious but less enchanting Pho Ngk. *Punto e bastà*.

A week passes.

The director reads fifteen other scripts (which he is also being paid to "develop.")

The indie-prod has called your agent, screaming that his client (i.e., you) lives on the immoral earnings of women; that he (you) will never work in this town again, etc.

The agent then calls you into his/her office, and you explain your love for Alceste. When you mention the director's desired changes, your agent says, "Hey, that'd make a *swell* comedy!" but you continue to state your objections. Realizing you are serious, the agent then calls the indie-prod and explains your position, but tells him that you still *love* the project, are *dying* to go to Bangkok, and won't take another assignment for six months, pending of course, the newly negotiated contract.

Unless the indie-prod is a basket case, you will never set foot in Thailand.

You certainly won't get more money.

But the prod is stuck. He knows he will have to hire another writer, which will cost more than your revisions. He will also have to pay for that writer to fly to Bangkok in order to interview Thai transvestite prostitutes. (For the director is now *convinced* he is right—perhaps because he has been offered a *sixteenth* film to develop, and is waiting to hear from *his* agent the steps of the deal.)

If the i-p has any brains at all, he will tell the director that he wants to go with the present script. (Believe it or not, this *does* sometimes happen.) Either the director must fall into line (this occasionally happens, too), or the indie-prod will look for a different director.

Odd as it may seem, directors are every bit as expendable as writers. But starting out with a new writer is expensive. (You've seen those films, the ones with four writers on the credits. Name *three* such films which are memorable.)

Obviously situations are rarely as extreme as this example.

But character change can mean theme change, idea change. Inevitably it means narrative change.

Fight.

Surrender.

Retreat.

Believe in yourself as a writer, and commit yourself fully to your work. In this way will you serve the project best. For if you begin to doubt yourself, the script blithely will follow those doubts. Frustration will join the funeral cortege, followed by anxiety and insomnia. And was it worth it? And for what?

*   *   *

Very well.

Now you know how to play Gary Cooper in the remake of *High Noon*. But can you take on the town or, at least, the structure of it, by yourself?

1. The Writers' Guild, and/or Your Agent

Unless the debacle concerns minimum wages, credit arbitration or disposition of payment, the Writers' Guild will be no help to you. Until screenwriters band together to force the Producers' Guild to accept the fact that *an original screenplay is the full and complete domain of the writer, and that no script changes can or will exist without the express approval of the author,* you will have to insist that your own agent negotiate the following conditions in your contract:

1. No script changes unless approved by the author.
2. The final word concerning those changes belongs to the author.
3. The author will co-produce the film, and have a voice equal to the producer's in the selection of director and cast.

This tells the indie-prod that you are prepared to stand behind your work in order to help him realize the fulfillment of your vision.

The charm of the indie-prod will be used to woo you into believing "*you'll have that choice anyway.*"

Wrong.

Get it in writing.

Your agent will tell you that no indie-prod will agree to those conditions.

Wrong again.

If the i-p wants your script, he/she will agree to most anything.

Be firm.

The original screenplay was your vision alone. Protect it. If it goes astray, you have only yourself to blame.

(As I have stated earlier, however, in the case of adaptations, the vision obviously is not yours; your role is that of craftsman; you have no right to make the same demands as you would with an original screenplay.)

Believe in your worth, your craft.

Protect your vision contractually.

As hard as this may be, in the course of your career the industry will learn to accept these conditions. Lord, but they've accepted far worse! (I remember one star insisting that the entire first class of an airplane be bought when he traveled to location—in order to carry his wife, children, two governesses, hairdresser, wardrobe-mistress, body guards, and masseur, all of whom were provided for contractually.)

Meanwhile, continue to lobby in the Writers' Guild for the author's full protection of an original screenplay.

2. Obey The Tee Shirt

If you dream your writing, then write your dreaming, why not consider giving the dream physical shape? In other words, direct your own work?

It is axiomatic in Europe that a writer eventually will direct his writing.

Film began that way, didn't it? The best of it has stayed that way.

Griffith, Mack Sennett, Chaplin, Renoir, Pabst, Bergman, Fellini, Truffaut, Woody Allen, all added to the vocabulary of film as they pursued their visions.

If you've dreamed the scene, then you certainly know its texture and rhythm better than anyone else.

Directing is not an end in itself.

Fully realizing your vision, your writing, *is*.

Take acting classes.

Direct scenes.

Learning how to move a camera is less difficult than learning how to work with performers. Your own writing will improve, and you will be presented with legitimate acting problems in your own work.

Go to theater.

Stay on the set of films.

Study writer-directors whose works you respect.

Once screenwriters take full responsibility for their visions, the state of the art will improve a thousandfold.

*   *   *

A lovely dream, surely, but impractical?

Not at all.

Here is how to do it:

Write a script you want to direct. Put it in your drawer. Show it to no one. When another film you have written is a hit, or your reputation becomes solid, pull out that script and have your agent act quickly, selling it *on the condition that you direct*.

You will be surprised how the indie-prods will fall into line.

Once this is done, get the prod to commit as much money as possible into pre-production. If he's spent $500,000 it will be more difficult for him to pull out than if he'd spent $50.00.

Odd as this may seem, it's done every day.

As of this writing, I have had eight contracts to direct my own screenplays. (Yet, as my friend Don Aquilino, the painter, had stated at the Rome track, when our 25-to-1 horse was eight lengths ahead and suddenly lost its saddle, "Why is it whenever we win, we *still* lose?" To which I replied, "Dammit, our *system* works! The *jockeys* don't!")

The eight contracts have faded into smog, or soggy pasta, yes.

But the ninth is just around the corner.

Time, luck, and probability theory—which means nothing less or more than *endurance*—eventually will tighten the saddle. A dose of anger and talmudic self righteousness also always helps.

And the knowledge that as studio heads roll, you will continue to write.

A Lament, Followed by a Miracle

Often, I have heard young film students complain, "Now that I know more about construction, I can see the tricks the author's using. I'll never just be able to sit back and enjoy a film again!"

That's too bad, really.

It implies that art was thought to be an honest affair.

When, I ask myself, has an affair *ever* been honest?

The muses are neither strict logicians nor moral philosophers. (What they *are* is left to your own experience. John Fowles's delightful musing, *Mantissa*, may well give you a clue to a muse's idea of "limited engagement," and of the games played as force attempts to coax idea into form, and as idea, no easy trick to coax, fights back, and with an arsenal of tricks far more potent than any author could devise!)

Suffice to say, reading a screenplay or viewing a film for an understanding of craft, of how a particular writer manipulates his audience, is not only enlightening, but also fun. For one thing, it tells you a great deal about the author, while demonstrating his legerdemain. (French for: lightness of hand.)

Art honest, indeed?

The idea may be as pure as Isolde's heart.

But the rest—the craft, the manipulation, the setting-up of expectations—would make Mme. Recamier herself turn away with polite (always polite) embarrassment.

To return to the students' complaint:

Relax.

No matter how much you think you've understood

the author's construction, if the fellow knows his stuff you *still* will be awed.

I have read Ennio Flaiano's extraordinary screenplay of *8½* as many times as I've seen the film, but the whole always remains greater than the sum of its much-studied parts. I have analyzed each canto of Dante's *Inferno* from a variety of perspectives—aesthetic, historical, religious—and I still cannot say what the poet has done to move me so deeply. More, I have studied the formal elements of fugue counterpoint and harmony, and yet I still find myself falling away from the rigors of analysis as I listen to Mozart's *Don Giovanni*, Bartok's *Concerto for Strings, Percussion, and Celeste,* or Dizzy Gillespie and Charlie Parker being Diz and Bird.

No matter how many times I have seen Botticelli's *Primavera* (as long as I'm worshipping muses), the painting itself remains the Eleventh Wonder of the World (Sappho's fragments being the Tenth).

Now I will tell you about a miracle, which of course is nothing less than an exception to the rule:

Several years ago a producer at M-G-M asked me to adapt Milton's *Paradise Lost*.

Yes.

What would *you* have done?

Here's what I did.

After picking my jaw off the floor, I asked the producer if he actually had *read* the poem.

"Well," he began, "I read a *treatment*. But there *was* a screenplay already written. I think I read that, too, but it doesn't work."

Logic would have dictated my asking, "But if you've not read the *original,* how could you have made the comparison?"

But there is nothing logical about the merry world of movies.

"The studio *says* it doesn't work," he continued.

"Please," I replied. "I don't think I'm the man to do justice to Milton's work. . . . By the way, whoever had the nerve to attempt an adaptation?"

"John Collier," replied the producer.

Now John Collier is an elegant author of macabre short stories. *Fancies and Goodnights* is a superlative collection of the genre.

I wondered.

"Send me his adaptation," I said.

How can anyone make a movie of *Paradise Lost*?

John Collier isn't anyone.

And he *did* adapt Milton's epic poem.

In fact, it is the finest adaptation I have ever read.

For Collier did what any intelligent and graceful writer would do: *he entered the adaptation through the language itself*, transforming the symphonic *cadences* in Milton's vision to provide him with the substance and texture of each scene; most importantly, *he translated Milton's imagery into movie image*.

Because I wanted to see Collier's adaptation filmed, I told the studio that I would agree to the changes they demanded. Since this occurred during the "swinging sixties," they wanted the epic "to be where it's *really* at."

This ostensible "updating," I countered, would consist of Collier's script, propped-up with modern parallels. (I didn't even know what I meant.) Without telling them my secret plan, I had hoped that the director would immediately eliminate my props, and shoot the substance, which was Collier's script.

Happily, the studio lost its chief.

Unhappily, *Capricorn One* was shot instead.

I told my bizarre adventure to a friend who knows John Collier.

And several years later I received a book in the mail. A major publisher had brought out a hardbound edition of Collier's screenplay. With it was a note from the adapter:

"For Stephen Geller—but for whom this screenplay never would have been published.—John Collier."

Writing is not a secure profession. (I laugh as I write this line.) Screenwriting even less. But if you are mad enough to inflict your dreams upon the unsuspecting public, then learn to inflict them well, and to control the direction of the infliction.

Screenwriting and other forms of sadomasochism can be fun.

But don't say I didn't warn you.

ABOUT THE AUTHOR

Stephen Geller has earned his living as a screenwriter for the past fifteen years. He has written scripts for SLAUGHTERHOUSE-FIVE, THE VALACHI PAPERS, LUNATICS AND LOVERS, ASHANTI, SEE NO EVIL, MR. AMBASSADOR, EVEN COWGIRLS GET THE BLUES, and TROY TALK. Mr. Geller has also written four novels: SHE LET HIM CONTINUE (which became the four-star movie PRETTY POISON starring Anthony Perkins and Tuesday Weld), PIT BULL, JOOP'S DANCE, GAD, and PEDULUM, a nonfiction work, will appear in late 1984. He has been a contributing editor to the *National Lampoon* and has contributed reviews to the *New York Times* and the *Saturday Review of Literature*. A graduate of Dartmouth College and the Yale School of Drama, he is a Visiting Professor in the Dartmouth Film Studies program. Mr. Geller lives in Rome with his wife and daughters.

Facts at Your Fingertips!

☐ 24433	DOING IT NOW	$3.50
☐ 23522	GETTING THINGS DONE	$3.50
☐ 24128	THE ART OF FUND RAISING	$3.50
☐ 23595	THE ART OF MIXING DRINKS	$3.50
☐ 24145	THE BANTAM BOOK OF CORRECT LETTER WRITING	$3.95
☐ 23474	AMY VANDERBILT'S EVERYDAY ETIQUETTE	$3.95
☐ 24968	SOULE'S DICTIONARY OF ENGLISH SYNONYMS	$3.95
☐ 22898	THE BANTAM NEW COLLEGE SPANISH & ENGLISH DICTIONARY	$2.95
☐ 23990	THE GUINNESS BOOK OF WORLD RECORDS 22nd ed.	$3.95
☐ 24841	IT PAYS TO INCREASE YOUR WORD POWER	$3.50
☐ 25237	THE BANTAM COLLEGE FRENCH & ENGLISH DICTIONARY	$3.95
☐ 24974	SCRIBNER/BANTAM ENGLISH DICTIONARY	$3.50
☐ 22974	WRITING AND RESEARCHING TERM PAPERS	$2.95

Prices and availability subject to change without notice.

Buy them at your local bookstore or use this handy coupon for ordering:

Bantam Books, Inc., Dept. RB, 414 East Golf Road, Des Plaines, Ill. 60016

Please send me the books I have checked above. I am enclosing $_____
(please add $1.25 to cover postage and handling). Send check or money order
—no cash or C.O.D.'s please.

Mr/Mrs/Miss _____

Address _____

City_____State/Zip_____

RB—5/85

Please allow four to six weeks for delivery. This offer expires 11/85.

SPECIAL
MONEY SAVING
OFFER

Now you can have an up-to-date listing of Bantam's hundreds of titles plus take advantage of our unique and exciting bonus book offer. A special offer which gives you the opportunity to purchase a Bantam book for only 50¢. Here's how!

By ordering any five books at the regular price per order, you can also choose any other single book listed (up to a $4.95 value) for just 50¢. Some restrictions do apply, but for further details why not send for Bantam's listing of titles today!

Just send us your name and address plus 50¢ to defray the postage and handling costs.

BANTAM BOOKS, INC.
Dept. FC, 414 East Golf Road, Des Plaines, Ill 60016

Mr./Mrs./Miss/Ms. _____
(please print)

Address _____

City_____ State_____ Zip_____

FC—3/84

We Deliver!
And So Do These Bestsellers.

☐	24964	**JERUSALEM, SONG OF SONGS** by Jill & Leon Uris	$4.95
☐	24874	**PREVIEWS AND PREMISES** by Alvin Toffler	$3.95
☐	24649	**FUTURE SHOCK** by Alvin Toffler	$4.95
☐	24698	**THE THIRD WAVE** by Alvin Toffler	$4.95
☐	24364	**DESTINY & 102 OTHER REAL LIFE MYSTERIES** by Paul Aurandt	$3.50
☐	20893	**PAUL HARVEY'S THE REST OF THE STORY**	$2.95
☐	24842	**MORE OF PAUL HARVEY'S THE REST OF THE STORY** by Paul Aurandt	$3.50
☐	34094	**800 COCAINE** by Mark S. Gold, M.D.	$2.95
☐	05064	**WITNESS TO WAR** by Dr. Charles Clements (A Bantam Hardcover)	$15.95
☐	23792	**THE COP WHO WOULDN'T QUIT** by Johnny Bonds & Rick Nelson	$3.95
☐	24846	**THE UMPIRE STRIKES BACK** by R. Luciano	$3.95
☐	05049	**STRIKE TWO** by R. Luciano (A Bantam Hardcover)	$14.95
☐	25225	**TOUGHLOVE** by P. & D. York w/ T. Wachtel	$3.95
☐	05042	**HEARTS WE BROKE LONG AGO** by M. Shain (A Large Format Book)	$10.95
☐	22646	**SOME MEN ARE MORE THAN PERFECT** by Merle Shain	$2.95
☐	22649	**WHEN LOVERS ARE FRIENDS** by Merle Shain	$2.95
☐	24304	**YOUR ACHING BACK** by A. A. White III, M.D.	$3.95
☐	23029	**HAVING IT BOTH WAYS** by E. Denholtz	$3.50
☐	23568	**GET A JOB IN 60 SECONDS** by Steve Kravette	$2.95
☐	23563	**THE ONLY INVESTMENT GUIDE YOU'LL EVER NEED** by Andrew Tobias	$3.95

Prices and availability subject to change without notice.

Buy them at your local bookstore or use this handy coupon for ordering:

Bantam Books, Inc., Dept. NFB, 414 East Golf Road, Des Plaines, Ill. 60016

Please send me the books I have checked above. I am enclosing $_____
(please add $1.25 to cover postage and handling). Send Check or money
—no cash or C.O.D.'s please.

Mr/Mrs/Miss _____

Address_____

City_____ State/Zip_____

NFB—5/85

Please allow four to six weeks for delivery. This offer expires 11/85.